R·NO-4
215
AF592704

Dr. Ram Manohar Lohia

About the Author

Dr. Sarbjit Singh Chhina is Ph.D. in Agricultural Economics. He retired as Dean, Faculty of Agriculture, Khalsa College, Amritsar, a prestigious institution in India. He was also Head, Deptt. of Economics and Sociology. During his academic career, he had been member of the Senate and Syndicate of Guru Nanak Dev University. He had been member of the faculty of Agriculture and Forestry, Member, Board of Studies of Economics and Business, and member of other academic societies and associations. He is honorary Director of Indian Institute of Industrial Economics and Development Society. He is also Editor of the 'Indian Journal of Industrial Economics and Development'. He had written a number of books in the field of Economics. Some of his books on Agricultural Economy are prescribed throughout the colleges and universities of India. He is associated with many educational, cultural, social and sports organizations like Indian Red Cross Society, Indian Academy of Fine Arts, Confederation of UNESCO Clubs in India. He is a regular contributor to the popular newspapers on the Economic Issues.

Dr. Ram Manohar Lohia

A Veteran Socialist

Sarbjit Singh Chhina

CONCEPT PUBLISHING COMPANY PVT. LTD.
NEW DELHI-110059

© Dr. Sarbjit Singh Chhina

All rights reserved. No part of this work may be reproduced, stored, adapted, or transmitted in any form or by any means, electronic, mechanical, photocopying, micro-filming recording or otherwise, or translated in any language, without the prior written permission of the copyright owner and the publisher. The book is sold subject to the condition that it shall not, by way of trade or otherwise, be lent, resold, hired out, or otherwise circulated without the prior publisher's written consent in any form of binding or cover other than that in which it is published.

The views and opinions expressed in this book are author(s) own and the facts reported by him/her have been verified to the extent possible, and the publishers are not in any way liable for the same.

ISBN-13 : 978-81-8069-922-1

First Published 2013

Published and Printed by

Concept Since 1974

Concept Publishing Company Pvt. Ltd.
A/15-16, Commercial Block, Mohan Garden
New Delhi-110059 (India)
T: 25351460, 25351794, *F*: 091-11-25357109
E: publishing@conceptpub.com, W: www.conceptpub.com
Editorial Office: H-13, Bali Nagar, New Delhi-110 015, India.

Cataloging in Publication Data--*Courtesy:* D.K. Agencies (P) Ltd. <docinfo@dkagencies.com>

Chhina, S. S. (Sarbjit Singh)
Dr. Ram Manohar Lohia : a veteran socialist / Sarbjit Singh Chhina.
p. cm.
Includes index.
ISBN 9788180699221

1. Lohia, Rammanohar. 2. Nationalists—India—Biography. 3. Socialists—India Biography. 4. India—Politics and government—20th century. 5. India—Social conditions. I. Title.

DDC 954.042092 23

Foreword

Let me at the outset congratulate the author Dr. S.S. Chhina for writing this book on Dr. Ram Manohar Lohia. The younger generations will benefit immensely from reading such books on the lives of heroes of the freedom struggle. The sacrifices and sufferings of these freedom fighters. Some known and vast number of unknown, under the unique leadership of Gandhiji, have contributed to the realization of the dream of independence of India.

I have had a good fortune to be close to Dr. Lohia as he was a very dear friend of my father Shri P.Y. Deshpande. We have had many occasions to have him as our guest at our Nagpur residence and long informal discussions with him. Listening to him was like reading the chapters from the book of freedom movement. He had shared many anecdotes of Mahatma Gandhi and others, with us.

I would like to recommend this book for libraries, schools, colleges, universities, etc., so that it may be read by large number of people. Dr. Lohia was more concerned with economic prosperity of the country, social justice and moral values. As a socialist, he wanted all distinctions between man and man, caste, class, creed, gender, etc. should go and every human being be treated as human being with all opportunity to live a life with honour. Dr. Chhina, M.A., Ph.D., a specialist in economics, has written the biography about Dr. Ram Manohar Lohia, characterized by his scholarship and painstaking research. I convey my good wishes to Dr. Chhina.

New Delhi-110 003
3rd July, 2005

Nirmala Deshpande
Member of Parliament
(Rajya Sabha)

Contents

Introduction

Dr. Ram Manohar Lohia was undoubtedly the most original thinker, and, perhaps, the only one produced in India during the last hundred odd years. Unlike most thinkers whose thought remains encapsuled for others to act upon, Lohia was a man of action who paid a heavy price for the courage of his convictions, having been arrested and jailed on innumerable occasions by the governments of Britain, India, Portugal, Nepal and the United States. He was also a political seer whose foresight into events always put him in a situation of being at least twenty years ahead of his time. Perhaps it is this prophet in him which once made him say: 'People will listen to me. Perhaps, after I am dead. But they will certainly listen to me'.

And people are listening to Dr. Lohia in India and outside nearly twenty years after he is dead.

At some point of time, Lohia summed up the essence of the great struggles in which humanity was engaged in the middle of the twentieth century, and of which he and the Socialist Party he had helped to create were a part. The Seven Revolutions, as he called them, were:

1. For equality between man and woman;
2. Against political, economic and spiritual inequality based on skin colour;
3. Against inequality of backward and high groups or castes based on long tradition, and for giving special opportunities to the backward;
4. Against foreign enslavement and for freedom and world democratic rule;
5. For economic equality and planned production and against the existence of and attachment for private capital;
6. Against unjust encroachments on private life and for democratic methods; and
7. Against weapons and for *satyagraha*.

It is around these struggles or revolutions that Lohia weaved his thoughts and programmes, constantly spearheading movements that earned him the opprobrium of the upholders of the old order which these struggles sought to overturn. The media in India, and for that matter the world over, which has generally been the handmaiden when it is not the whiplash of the ruling establishment, went to great lengths to denounce and denigrate Lohia like no other public personality in the country, through the clever subterfuge of distortion and the projection of the shadow but seldom the substance of what he said or did.

For all the efforts of some savants of political history to trace the beginnings of socialism in vedic literature and in the teachings of Jesus Christ, socialism is an idea that is of recent origin, the word itself making its first appearance around 1830. While many thinkers and writers in Europe produced among themselves varying themes of the same idea, often laced with the Christian ethic, it was Karl Marx who proceeded to synthesise these themes into his theory of scientific socialism. The First International founded in 1864 was used by Marx to spread his ideas as distinct from those whom he chose to brand as utopian socialists. But scientific or utopian, all socialists strongly believed in the international brotherhood of the working people whose united strength would ultimately break the chains which bound them. The First International had been dissolved in 1876 and the Second International founded in 1889. And by now the socialists were emerging as the most significant political force in Europe, more convinced than ever that the future lay with the workers of the world.

It was the First World War that destroyed all dreams (or were they illusions?) of socialist universalism, when the workers took up arms not to destroy their oppressors and exploiters but to defend their respective father or mother-lands, ruled by the very oppressors against whom they were fighting till the day before. With the death of the dream of the brave new world, what remained was the hope that socialism would provide the working people with better standards of living through the capture of power whether through parliamentary or other means. Between the Russian revolution and the Second World War with Hitler and other fascist leaders holding the centre stage in Europe, Lohia was studying at the Berlin University and was a ringside spectator of the cataclysmal developments that made a mockery of socialist and working class internationalism. And that is where he must have begun his search for truth which not only made him an inveterate foe of all dogma, Marxist or any other, and an iconoclast, but also a person who doggedly sought to marry precept with practice, both at personal and political levels.

Lohia's rejection of capitalism and communism was rooted in his intellectual perception of the "community of economic aims" they both shared and in their inadequacy to deal with the problems of large sections of humanity. He was unable to reconcile with those who believed that communism created conditions for economic democracy while capitalism allowed political democracy to flower. Lohia asserted that "communism (inherited) from capitalism its technique of production; it only (sought) to smash the capitalist relations of production", and went on to point out that communism claimed to be the continuator and developer of capitalist technology when capitalism itself was no longer able to do so.

To Lohia, socialism was a "newer doctrine than capitalism or communism", which had to devise its own ideological and pragmatic formulations that could chart a new course to liberate humanity from the misery into which capitalism had pushed it. The evolution of European socialism into some kind of welfare statism had already convinced Lohia of its irrelevance to nearly two-thirds of the world whose economics had been ravaged by world capitalism. If European socialists had achieved distributed justice through constitutional methods applied gradually over a period of time, Lohia wanted socialism to be "drastic, unconstitutional when necessary, and lay the accent on production".

And it is in the area of production that Lohia propounded his theory of the small unit technology. Arguing that given the population densities in countries inhabited by the coloured people and their "woefully meagre" productive apparatus as compared to that of the white people of the world, it would be inconceivable for them to imitate the production patterns developed by capitalism, Lohia pleaded for "a new mode of rationalism and a corresponding mode of ownership" for the coloured people of the world. He wanted science to be concerned with the environment as with the people it sought to serve. Improving on Mahatma Gandhi's ideas of decentralized technology, Lohia wanted the invention and production of machines which would be available in towns and villages. "This immediacy in science and planning", as he called it, had to be matched with "immediacy in ownership and political control".

Lohia believed that the "vast agrarian masses of India, except the big landlords, are the builders of socialism, one and for all of them", and he decried the cavalier manner in which traditional socialism had treated the farmer. "European socialism and communism have drawn their main strength from the vast masses of factory workers and they have disliked the farmer, both because he is an owner of property and an exacter of high prices for their food", he wrote. If the western theory of the factory worker being the sole agency of the revolution was absurd, so was the one that sought to elevate the farmer into the sole instrument of the new order. According to Lohia: Undoubtedly, the farmer in India, as elsewhere, has a great role to play, than no one is greater, but others may have equal roles to play. The talk of subsidiary alliances between farmers and workers and artisans and the city poor must be replaced by the concept of equal relationships in the revolution.

The struggle for this new political and economic order, however, had to be a peaceful one, though Lohia did not rule out spontaneous violence at a certain stage of an intense struggle by the people. While Gandhiji mystified his concept of *satyagraha*, Lohia called for individual and mass civil disobedience against injustice in all its forms and for the creation of a new order.

Lohia believed that unless the spirit of the Indian people which had declined over the centuries was revived, there would be no genuine forward movement for the country. "I am convinced that two segregation have enough power to kill all capacity for adventure and joy", he wrote. Stating that poverty and these two segregation thrived on each other's worms, he asserted that "all war on poverty is a sham, unless it is, at the same time, a conscious and sustained war on those two suggestions". It is this insight into the social situation in India which made him devise his theory of special opportunities or preferential treatment to the socially deprived sections of humanity. In the Socialist Party which was founded in 1955, sixty per cent of all offices and committees had to be filled by electing people who belonged to the Scheduled Castes, Scheduled

Tribes, Backward Castes, backward castes among minorities and women. He applied the same rule for all elective positions from parliament down to the local bodies.

This idea of preferential opportunities invited for Lohia the wrath of the Indian Establishment which has been and is still dominated by the upper castes. Lohia was aware of the odds he faced while seeking to give a real meaning to the abstract concept of equality in the specific Indian context, where five thousand years of history had condemned over eighty per cent of the people to a life of secondary status. He met the arguments of the Marxist dogmatists who were vicious in their attack on his concept of preferential opportunities and accused him of indulging in casteist politics by telling them that class was nothing but ossified caste.

Lohia believed that women in India suffered from two handicaps. One, from the usual, universal male domination. Two, and more important, from the obnoxious caste system. Therefore, it was all the more necessary that women were given special opportunities if they were ever to achieve equality with men in the Indian situation. "All politics in the country, Congress, Communist or Socialist, has one big area of national agreement, whether by design or through custom, and that is to keep down and disenfranchise the *sudra* and the woman who constitute over three-fourths of our entire population", he wrote in 1953.

While he appreciated and supported the concerns of urban feminists, he felt that the problems of women went far beyond matters like marriage and property rights.

According to Lohia: "The problem of the majority of Indian women is the lack of water taps and latrines. The Indian women are condemned to the drudgery of drawing water often dirt and muddy from distant wells or ponds and carry it home every morning and evening. She must also save her modesty by easing herself in the open fields either before sunrise or after sunset. Her slavery in the kitchen is an abomination, and the stove that smokes horribly". These became the issues of his campaigns and struggles for women's emancipation. At the same time, he wanted women to be involved in the agitation against under-feeding and unemployment and other injustices. Any talk of radical changes without women being involved in the struggles did not impress him. He once wrote: "I was a part of a coffee-house group of talkers. One day, when someone suggested that it was such coffee-talk that bred the French Revolution I boiled with rage. There was not one *sudra* among us. There was not one woman among us. A dull, effete and insipid lot we were, cattle ever cuddling yesterday's feed".

Lohia believed that for democracy to be real, the use of people's languages was *sine qua non*. The stranglehold of English had to be broken and children taught in their mother-tongue. Here again, he was as up against the power of the microscopic minority of English-read people who had acquired a grip on services and industry, even if their denial of people's languages was destroying the very soul of India. He warned against the deadly combination of the power of money, the English Language and upper caste in India's life.

The failure of the socialist movement to create an adequate enough instrument to spearhead the seven revolutions frustrated Lohia. But, unlike his comrade-in-arms, Jaya Prakash Narayan, who was so overwhelmed by the enormity of the task of taking socialism to power that he chose to withdraw himself into the world of non-party politics, Lohia soldiered on, prodding socialists to organize themselves into a party capable of capturing power in seven years, even while exhorting them to have patience and commitment to carry on the struggle for one hundred years.

The Chinese aggression in 1962 made Lohia change his tactical line of going it alone in the struggle for political power. He persuaded the entire spectrum of opposition parties to have mutual adjustments to overthrow Congress rule. The new tactical line on non-Congressism paid rich dividends in the elections to Parliament and the State Assemblies in January 1967, and Lohia was acknowledged as the tallest among all political leaders in the country. His death in October of the same year "caused by medical and governmental negligence", as Madhu Limaye put it, was a setback not only to the socialist movement but to the entire country.

While there is no reason to doubt that Indian history would have taken a different course if Lohia had survived a little longer, who knows if he would have lived to see his dreams converted into reality or died a sad and disillusioned man like Mahatma Gandhi before him and Jaya Prakash Narayan after him. But Lohia's thought will remain and acquire greater relevance as humanity grapples

with the myriad crises facing it and pursues the seven revolutions that Lohia had identified.

October 1, 2004 **George Fernandes**
Defence Minister

Childhood and Schooling

Nobody knew that Ram Manohar Lohia, born in a small village of Akbarpur, would become the main centre of opposition parties in the Centre and he would be the tallest and most important leader of the opposition. Being a leader of the opposition, the popularity and importance as gained by him, had perhaps never been available even to the ruling party leaders in any democracy. Although he was a leader of the opposition, yet the place of significance he enjoyed might not have been available to him even by becoming a Cabinet Minister or the Prime Minister of the country. As a result of his sway, the Government was more concerned about Dr. Lohia than the leaders of its own party. Not only the leaders of the ruling party, but even the Prime Minister and the President of India would become conscious of his statements made in rallies, in Parliament or even published in the Press. It was the general opinion of the public that if Dr. Lohia had not been a check on the Government, the ruling party might have felt that it could do anything it liked.

Ram Manohar made every possible effort for establishing such a social system which was neither like the capitalism that exploits the labourers nor like one-party rule of communists. He dreamt of establishing a socialist system in which the gap between incomes was minimum and there was economic, social and political equality and freedom of speech. To establish such a society he struggled before and after independence and laid its foundations. Before that, Indian politics and ideology was directed only towards two types of economic systems, i.e., the capitalist system which was prevalent at that time and was adopted by most of the countries of the world and the socialist system, which was introduced by the communists, where all the means of production belonged to the Government and everybody was a worker and was rewarded for the services rendered by him/her. In the capitalist system one can gather as much wealth as possible, whereas in socialist system of the communists, nobody could hold much wealth or employ someone else in one's enterprise.

Many books have been written on the ideology of Dr. Lohia. A large number of Research Centres and libraries have been established after his name. His followers live in every corner of the country and they are following his footsteps. Different political parties have adopted his ideology and at many times such parties have been partners in Government. It becomes necessary to study why his concepts are proper and why these attracted the attention of the world. Why were his writings and thoughts popular throughout the world? At present the communist system has come to an end in many countries and it is also being criticized. Lohia criticized that system when Soviet Russia was progressing rapidly under Communism and it was a big power. At that time Communism seemed practicable in all the countries of the world. Lohia challenged the Marxian interpretation of human history. Lohia believed that the unique weapon of Civil Disobedience and a few more aspects of Gandhian thought could be introduced profitably into Indian Socialism.

The great humanist, ideal socialist, maker of plans and programmes and devoted revolutionist, Ram Manohar Lohia, was born on March 23, 1910 in a small village named Akbarpur in the district of Faizabad (U.P.). His father Sh. Hira Lal was a man of progressive thoughts. He was a nationalist by spirit. His mother, Chanda, died when Ram was just a child. Shri Hira Lal loved his son very affectionately and wished to get him the best education for developing his all-round personality. However, there was no school as well as centre for promoting sports or cultural activities in his village. At that time most of the people of his village were illiterate and nobody was interested in the education of their children. The children used to help their parents in agriculture and later on they joined this job full-time. There was no provision of girls' education and neither was it considered important. Rather the girls remained confined to the four walls of their houses.

Lohia belonged to a well-to-do family having good source of income and social status. At one time, they were dealing in iron, that is why they became to be known as "Lohias", and this title "Lohia" became their identity. Being sharp-minded, Dr. Lohia was loved and appreciated by all the members of his family. His mother Chanda Ji belonged to Jhunjhunwala family of Chanpatia of Bihar. She was very careful about her son and she was always concerned to protect him from heat and cold. She spent most of her time to bathe and feed her beloved son. She unexpectedly passed away when Ram Manohar was only two and a half years old. Thereafter he lived under the affectionate care and guidance of his grandmother and aunt (sister of Hira Lal).

Hira Lal was the youngest amongst four sons of Shiv Kumar. They had a flourishing business in Mirzapur. However, after bearing a huge loss they left Mirzapur on the advice of Pandits.

Though Dr. Lohia could not get the love and affection of his mother, yet his grandmother and aunt fostered him so well that he could not live for a moment without them. They also provided him the love and affection of a mother. Both of them looked after him with utmost care keeping in mind the affection showered on him by his mother.

As the family began to prosper, Ram Manohar's education was given top priority. Simultaneously, due care was taken so that he might participate in games and other extra curricular activities for his all-round development. He got the love of a mother from his grandmother and aunt and he respected them throughout his life.

When he was only 5 years old, he was admitted in a school known as Tandon School near his village. He was very fond of playing games. Everybody thought that he would take less interest in education but contrary to the expectations he took keen interest in his studies. Though he was a brilliant student yet he took part in games and extra curricular activities.

After completing his primary education from Tandon School, Ram Manohar was admitted in Visheshwar Nath High School, situated near Akbarpur. Here again he pursued his studies very seriously. Reading was a passion with Dr. Lohia. His friends assert that had he not become a revolutionary, he would have become a bookworm and a university professor. He used to go school, with a very heavy bag of books wearing simple clothes. In school, during recess time, he was always surrounded by his class-mates and they would ask him a number of questions. It was very interesting and strange to note that even for philosophical questions his answers were so correct that his teachers too became surprised. Once his friend asked him a question, "What is this British Government". Lohia answered, "When there is no unity in a country then foreigners attack on that country and get its control". The answer of that question remained in the memory of his friends even in their old age.

For his Matric, Ram Manohar took admission in Marwari School, Bombay. At that time, his father had started a new business. Although his business was flourishing, yet he never wanted his son to join the business at the cost of his studies. He wanted his son to be fully educated. He used to write him letters twice a week, advising his son to be more careful about his health and studies. In these letters his affection and love for his beloved child was clearly visible. That showed his deep concern for the health and future prospects of his son. Ram Manohar himself was very much interested in pursuing his studies and he never thought about business as an alternative for education.

Ram Manohar continued to pursue studies with devotion and dedication. He also took keen interest in sports. Being impressed by these qualities, many of his classmates became his good friends. However, while studying in school he took special interest in history and politics of the country. It was because of the fact that his father was associated with the Congress Party and was contributing to the freedom struggle of thc country. In 1918, the session of the Congress Party was held at Allahabad. His father took Ram Manohar with him, as he wanted to be with his son for a long time. At the same time, he wanted to show him Allahabad, a big city, and to make him aware of the political activities of the country. It was a new experience for Ram Manohar. The people wearing white "khaddar" were looking very pretty. Ram Manohar very attentively listened to the speech of every leader and on the same night, he put his father so many questions. Ram was introduced to the Indian freedom struggle at an early age by his father through the various protest assemblies. Ram made his first contribution to the freedom struggle by organizing a small *hartal* on the death of Lok Manya Tilak.

Lok Manya Tilak departed for heavenly abode in August 1920. People from all over India reached Bombay to pay homage to their beloved leader. On that occasion, the leadership qualities of Dr. Lohia emerged for the first time. He led the students of his school in the form of a procession for paying homage to Lok Manya Tilak. Gandhiji too entered into politics in the same year and people welcomed this move. Unfortunately, in 1921, grandmother of Dr. Lohia expired. It was a matter of great sorrow for Ram Manohar as he got the love and affection of a mother from her. After reaching Akbarpur, he became very sad recollecting the moments spent with his grandmother. After some days Nehruji came to Faizabad and he stayed in the house of Lohias. Ram Manohar became very much impressed by his sterling personality. Lohia attended the Congress session of 1924 as a delegate, though at that time he was only a teenager. Lohia passed his Matric from Bombay University in 1925 with first division.

Ram Manohar was in favour of continuing his studies. He was admitted in the prestigious Banaras Hindu University for his intermediate. He started wearing "khaddar" and felt the need of spectacles due to poor *visibility*. He used both these articles throughout his life. He completed his intermediate in the year of 1927. In those days, most of the people studied up to intermediate level only and after that, they used to seek jobs. However, Ram Manohar joined Vidya Sagar College for his B.A. (Honours) in English. He attended a session of the Congress Party in 1928 and impressed all the leaders with his towering personality. Therefore, they were attracted towards him. Due to his sharp mind, some trusts/institutions offered him fellowships so that he might continue his higher studies. He belonged to a rich family. So money was not a big problem for him. However, such offers encouraged him and he started taking more interest in his studies. His psyche was deeply hurt when he came to know that a great personality and warrior like Shivaji had been mentioned as a dacoit in some of the books.

During those early years of his life, he was influenced by the great personality of his father. His father wrote him letters frequently and through every letter advised him to be careful about health. At that time, there was a practice of remarriage for widowers. But Hira Lal did not accept such suggestions because of his deep love and affection for his son. He was determined not to marry again throughout his life. He created the political inclination in Ram Manohar by taking him along at the sessions of the Congress.

The Congress session of 1928 was presided over by Moti Lal Nehru. In that conference, a number of responsibilities were entrusted to Dr. Lohia. Outside the Congress Hall, Nehru had a meeting with Ram Manohar. Being impressed by the inspiring personality of Lohia, Nehru nicknamed him as the "young king". He had the quality to create eternal friendship. At that time he had a number of friends. He was very fond of taking *"gol gappa" chat*, etc. in the company of his friends. He was in the habit of having friendly chat with his friends till late night and after that, he used to burn midnight oil for his studies. However, lying on his bed, he liked to have the fond memories of his father, his grandmother, all his childhood friends, and his house at village Akbarpur. As he used to go to bed late at night, it was but natural that he was a late-riser. He was an office bearer of All India Students Organisation but many a time he had been warned for it.

In 1928, when Simon Commission arrived in India, Lohia was just 18 years old. However, even at that young age, he arranged a secret meeting of the students to propagate against that Commission and also managed to demonstrate their protest. Simon Commission was opposed throughout the country. In the same year, Jawahar Lal Nehru organised a youth conference at Calcutta that was presided over by Nehru himself. Ram Manohar entrusted different duties to a number of young men to make that conference a big success. At that time, Subhash Chander Bose was the President of the Subject Committee and Ram Manohar was its member. After having a discussion with Ram Manohar, Subhash Chander Bose was very much influenced by Lohia's distinguished personality and he remarked that one day he would play a major role in the politics of the country.

To go Abroad for the sake of Education

In those days, only the children of princes, jagirdars and very rich persons had the resources for going abroad to pursue higher studies. Most of these children used to go abroad to seek admission in the universities/colleges of London. However, the middle class families were not in a position to afford this huge expenditure. Though Lohia did not belong to a rich family, yet he managed to go to London for higher studies. He did not like London and particularly the behaviour of the Britishers. Mr. Ziradar became his close friend in London. Lohia expressed him his views of leaving London. Zirader was very much impressed by his innocent behaviour. He continuously persuaded him not to leave London. Nevertheless, Lohia was determined to leave England. So after some days, Lohia left England and joined the University of Berlin in Germany.

While in Germany, he was in close touch with his family, particularly his father, who was much worried for his future and used to advice him through letters. Through letters Dr. Lohia was also having the information about the political and social life of India. Thus, he became deeply concerned with the economic life of the masses of his beloved country. Although Lohia got political tinge from his family, yet his vision about politics was widened in Germany.

In those days, Germany was facing many economic problems. Hitler was rising as a political hero of that country. At one side, Germans were creating much hatred for the Britishers; on the other side, Indians were struggling for their independence. Germans were having sympathies for the Indians. In this context, Lohia gave many speeches to the students and teachers of Germany. He explained them the real state of affairs of Indian politics.

On March 6, 1930, Gandhiji broke the Salt Act, which was enacted by the Britishers in India. That incident was the headlines of the newspapers throughout the world. As a result, demonstrations were held in the different cities in India. Congress Leader Mrs. Sarojini Naidu also led one of the processions. Police resorted to lathi charge and many people were injured due to the high-handedness of the police. Some of them went into coma due to injuries. Hira Lal was also hurt in that procession. Therefore, he wrote a letter to his son wherein he mentioned the simmering condition of the country. In the meantime, unfortunately, S. Bhagat Singh was hanged on March 23 and Ram Manohar Lohia became very disturbed to hear this news.

Burner Jambart, a famous contemporary economist, was the teacher of Ram Manohar in the Berlin University. Lohia was granted degree of Ph.D. in 1932 on the topic "Salt and Civil Disobedience".

Subsequently a meeting of the League of Nations was held in London. Maharaja of Bikaner represented India in that convention. As Maharaja of Bikaner was a supporter of the British Government, so it was presumed that he would naturally support the policies of the British Government. Dr. Lohia, somehow managed to enter in the Meeting Hall, and as soon as the Maharaja stood up to speak, Ram Manohar started to whistle. But he was immediately overpowered, manhandled and thrown out of the Hall. On the next day, he wrote a letter to the President of the League of Nations and simultaneously he sent its copies to the newspapers. The letter was under the heading of "Lack of Humanity" and it contained the facts which proved that the views of Maharaja Bikaner were not correct. That letter appeared in the various newspapers. On the next day, he purchased a number of newspapers and stood at the gate of the hall. After some time, he started distributing the newspapers to the people entering the Hall. In this way, Lohia got the attraction of the people. He also formed a Middle Europe-Indian Association and he himself became its patron and secretary. He was growing as a popular socialist.

Meanwhile, Gandhi-Irwin Pact was signed but that was vehemently opposed by the communists and Middle Europe-Indians Association. However, Ram Manohar stood in favour of Gandhiji and opposed the communist arguments. He supported the agreement struck between Gandhi and Irwin as a step towards the welfare of the Indians. During this turmoil, Hitler was unanimously accepted as the ruler of Germany.

In 1933, at the time of his return to India, he packed a lot of books. But as he had become a popular leader and

German Government considered him as their opponent, the authorities confiscated all his material assets and he was sent empty handed. He boarded a ship and reached Madras. He bowed his head to his motherland. In Madras, he had no money. Moreover, he had no friend or relative over there who could help him. But in his own country, he was greatly satisfied and was having eternal bliss. From Madras Lohia was to reach Calcutta immediately for his further programmes but he had no money to meet the travelling expenses. He approached the Deputy Editor of the newspaper *The Hindu*. He wrote an article for that paper and was paid Rs. 25 as remuneration. Dr. Lohia went to his friend who made arrangements for his journey to Calcutta.

In Germany, while pursuing his studies, Lohia had become familiar with the history of the different countries and historical knowledge of different cultures. Many a time, he compared the human rights available to the European people with the rights being enjoyed by the Indian people. Every time he felt that in India 80 per cent people were not aware of their human rights. He compared the slavery of his countrymen with the freedom of the citizens of European countries. This thinking increased his rancour for the Britishers and he began to find a way out for the freedom of his country. On reaching Calcutta, Dr. Lohia was informed that Gandhiji had been arrested on his way back from England after attending the Round Table Conference. It further hurt his psyche and he thought to demonstrate the protest in a large scale. Gandhiji's arrest was followed by public protests all over the country and a number of people were arrested. The police began to perpetuate atrocities on the general masses which deeply hurt his psyche. He pitied the plight and helplessness of the people of his country.

After Return to India

While studying in Germany, Ram Manohar had made up his mind not to compete either for I.C.S. or for any other Government job in India. Reaching back to India, he observed that the business of his father had failed miserably. It was due to the fact that he could not devote sufficient time for his business and remained busy in different activities concerning the freedom struggle. However, he noticed that his father was neither worried nor was feeling any regrets for that. Dr. Lohia also noticed that his father was following the preaching enshrined in *Bhagvad Gita* and used to devote his maximum time for Congress activities. He advised his beloved son to be content and satisfied even in the adverse circumstances without leaving the path of virtuousness, self-respect, morality and social values. Though at that time his family was facing great hardship due to poverty, yet Dr. Lohia was determined that he would not seek any Government job. He was interested in teaching profession and it was very surprising that he could not secure a teaching job even after having such a higher degree. However, he was offered some lucrative jobs in private companies but those did not match Lohia's taste.

Therefore, he refused to do such jobs. Meanwhile he went to meet his old friend Mr. Ram Ji Kaushal at his residence. He was a professor who disliked cigarette smoking. Ram Manohar was aware of his hatred for cigarettes. Dr. Lohia was fond of cigarette smoking but he did not smoke as long as he stayed at the house of Prof. Kaushal. His friend arranged a speech of Ram Manohar Lohia in Teachers' Training College. The teachers and the students became very much impressed by his lecture. Shri Madan Mohan Malviya was interested to get him appointed as Professor of Economics in Banaras Hindu University but he could not succeed in his efforts. Then a big industrialist of that time, Mr. Rameshwar Dass Birla offered him the job of his personal secretary. Though the post was not of his taste, yet he accepted it.

Ram Manohar was having hatred for the British Empire as well as for the capitalists of that time because that had created the inequality in the economic and social life of the country. Lohia was closely watching the policies of Congress that was the prominent political party of that time. However, he was not in favour of the policies of the Congress. He was in favour of adopting a socialistic system of society but the Congress leaders were not agreed to this point. Meanwhile, after some time he left his job and went back to Calcutta.

Many relatives of Ram Manohar suggested for his marriage. However, Ram Manohar was determined not to marry throughout his life. His father who loved him most also wanted him to marry at this age though at the same time he encouraged his son to continue with his political activities. He persuaded Ram Manohar to get married, as he was growing old. Nevertheless, Ram Manohar put his strong arguments before his father that his life was full of uncertainties and he might face imprisonment, exile and even hanging. So he did not want to put another family on the doldrums and preferred to remain alone. His father accepted his arguments with heavy heart and afterwards never insisted his son to marry. Dr. Lohia was thinking over the plans to eradicate the poverty, hunger, diseases and inequality of wealth and income. He dreamt for such a society where equal opportunities and human rights are available to everyone. He wished that his party might launch a struggle to establish a socialist system.

He had a feeling that his fellow citizens should have no economic worries. Everybody must get employment and enjoy comforts and luxuries of life. He thought to make efforts for establishing a welfare state. For achieving this goal he planned to do anything that might promote the welfare of the society.

In 1934, the Congress Socialist Party was formed. Ram Manohar joined the same and became its full-time worker. Keeping in view his past performance, qualification and his views about socialism, he was also nominated as a member of the executive of the party. He was also appointed as the first editor of a journal *Congress Socialism* which was being published by the Congress Socialist Party. He took interest in international affairs and everyone liked his views. That is why he was appointed as the Secretary of the International wing of the party in 1935. Therefore, he had to change his office from Calcutta to Ahmedabad.

However, he had no residence. He was overloaded with work and used to sleep on the tables of the office. Afterwards he shifted his residence to the trade union centre but that was without the facilities of bathroom and toilet. Although the place of his residence was a consideration and that was affecting his efficiency, yet he never bothered about this inconvenience and continued with his work from morning till late in the evening. Later on, he shifted in the house of his friend in Mirzapur Street.

In those days, Mr. Jatin was one of his close friends. He had a tea-stall and used to provide breakfast for Dr. Lohia. He was so impressed by his views that he started to respect Dr. Lohia considering to be a saint. Jatin became aware that Lohia was working for the welfare of humanity selflessly. Being overwhelmingly impressed by his character, Jatin sold out his tea-stall and became full-time worker of the party. Dr. Lohia had one more friend in the city who was very rich. On his repeated invitations, Dr. Lohia visited him along with Mr. Jatin. At the time of departure his friend gave Rs. 200 to Dr. Lohia. He purchased his clothes, a Gandhi cap and took Mr. Jatin to a very costly hotel on that day. They took their meals and returned on a horse driven tonga. Still he was having Rs. 30. He thought to spend that money in a proper way. Next day he gave that money to the wife of a political worker who was in jail.

He was having another friend who belonged to Dacca. One day he came to know through telegram that his mother was ill. He was not having enough money for meeting travelling expenses. However, he managed the money sent his friend to Dacca. On that night, Ram Manohar suffered from nostalgia and began to think about his grandmother. In that context, he was also worried about the health of his friend's mother. He could not sleep whole of the night and the next morning he left for Dacca. His friend saw him surprisingly but at the same time, he was annoyed with him for having left the station in such an irresponsible way as the party had put on him a big responsibility. Anyhow, he arranged a speech of Ram Manohar in the Dacca University. The topic of the speech was "socialism". The students and professors of the University became very much impressed by that speech. Prof. J.L. Ghosh gave him Rs. 70 and that was enough money for their travelling expenses from Dacca to Calcutta.

The Congress was having two types of the views about its members. Some members were in favour of socialism whereas others were against it. In 1934, during the meeting of the working committee of Congress, this difference of opinion was plausible. Some of the party workers were in favour of elections as they wanted to be the members of the State Legislature but the socialists were against that move. A meeting of all the socialists of the country was called on May 17, 1934 at Calcutta to decide certain crucial issues. The meeting was presided over by Acharya Narender Dev and it was resolved to form a socialist party. It was also resolved to launch a socialist revolution for making the people aware about the socialist system and the aims of the socialist party. It was considered that if the party workers would be elected as members of the State Legislature, the struggle of freedom would become slow and weak. Hence, the resolution to establish the socialistic pattern of society was passed and Ram Manohar Lohia attached with it the resolution of complete freedom. Though Narender Dev supported his resolution but other leaders like Minoo Masani, Parshotam Das, Sampurnanand opposed that. Dr. Lohia was interested to establish a socialistic society at the earliest with complete freedom of the citizens. However, opposition in the party was a big hindrance on his way. It was thought that the party should have unanimous view. Therefore, because of the arguments put up by Jaya Prakash Narayan it was decided unanimously to postpone the resolution.

In the next meeting though Dr. Lohia and some other leaders were having different views, yet two resolutions were passed unanimously, viz., (1) Civil Disobedience and (2) to contest elections and enter in the State Legislatures.

Actually, Ram Manohar was never interested to gain any power while working in a political party. He was the first person with a state of mind "to serve the society through politics". He wished that that should be the aim of every politician. However, most of the leaders even before independence made the politics as a means to acquire power. Lohia was in favour of the selfless service of the society. Alas, it would have been the thinking of every politician!

In the same year on October 21 and 22 about 50 socialist leaders held a meeting at Bombay and announced to float a Congress Socialist Party. Lohia was the member of the executive of this party. Sampurnanand presided over this meeting. The next meeting of the party was held in Meerut in 1936. It was presided over by Kamalapati Chattopadhyay. Nevertheless, this time an amendment was made in the policies of the communist party at the international level and that affected the communists of India. In the meeting of Meerut, the communists were allowed to become members of the Congress socialist party but Lohia was not in its favour. Another Conference of the party also held in 1936 that was presided over by Jaya Prakash Narayan. In 1938, another session of the party was held at Lahore that was presided over by Minoo Masani and party was growing as a popular political party. The people liked the policies of the party.

On September 1937 in the Congress session at Allahabad, Lohia persuaded Indians not to participate in war and advised them to continue their struggle for the freedom of the country. In 1938, in Haripura session of the Congress, Lohia managed to pass the resolutions for the migrants in Mauritius, Fiji, China, Palestine, British Guiana, and Sri Lanka. He also managed to pass a resolution about the role of the party in Second World War.

Congress conference was held in Ramgarh in 1940 where it was decided that the membership of the communists should be removed. This move was taken because of the presumption that the communists of India were under the influence of Russia. By that time, Jawahar Lal Nehru and Jaya Prakash Narayan had returned from England and America respectively. Nehru said that Ram Manohar was the rising star. Inspite of the opposition of so many leaders he continued to be incharge of the foreign affairs of the party and by this time he had established relations with the organizations of 12 countries and got published some books. Those books became very popular. Some of the books are *China and India*, *India's Foreign Policy*, *The Exploitation of the Foreign Contractors*, and *The Struggle for Civil Liberties*, etc. He propagated the principles of socialism and civil liberties. At that time he wrote a number of articles and letters on the national and international economic and social issues and those were published in a number of newspapers.

Second World War

In those days, the war was going on in China, Japan, Italy and Abyssinia. League of Nations could not succeed to stop the war and the danger of the Second World War was increasing day-by-day and the socialists of India were worried about its consequences.

Many people were extending full support to the programmes of the Congress Socialist Party. Every non-professional was in favour of the Socialistic pattern of the society. The membership of the Socialist Party was growing in villages and all parts of the country. At that time Minoo Masani, Yusaf Mehar, Munshi Ahmad Din, Acharya Narender Dev, Shiv Nath Banerji, Ashok Mehta, Jaya Prakash Narayan, etc. were the prominent leaders of the party. An opinion was developing that there should be unity amongst all the socialists and communists. Many leaders of the party were in its favour but Ashok Mehta and Dr. Lohia were not in favour of such a unity. The main reason against this unity was that the communists in India were under the influence of Russian Communist Party. It was expected that they would act according to the instructions of their High Command, which would ultimately not be good for the country. However, because of the influence of Jaya Prakash Narayan they could not oppose it openly. In the Lahore session of 1938, the communists tried to capture one vacant seat of the National Executive but Ram Manohar Lohia was elected for that seat. In the same year, he left the office of the Secretary of International Wing of the Congress.

The Second World War broke out in 1939. Most of the countries of the world were divided in one or the other group. One group was led by England and the other was led by Germany. India was a part of the British Empire, so it was expected that its forces would fight for England. Indians were forced to join the war but India's struggle for independence had reached at a very crucial stage. Political leaders of India were also divided in two groups. One group was in favour of England while the other was against it. Dr. Ram Manohar was also of the opinion that the Indians and India's resources should not be used for the war of England. Rather India should continue its protest so that Englishmen might be compelled to leave India.

Ram Manohar made a number of speeches at the different places against the Britishers. As a result, the police started hunting him and he was arrested on May 24, 1939 from Calcutta. Afterwards, as per British policy, he was released from jail. This incident made no difference in his views and he continued to make the people aware about the atrocities being perpetrated on Indians by the Britishers. At that time, he was against Gandhi's views though he did not like the policy adopted by Subhash Chander Bose about the war.

Some of the Congress leaders including Subhash Chander Bose were of the view that maximum benefit of the war in Europe should be availed to intensify the freedom struggle. Ram Manohar also supported the views of Subhash Chander. But Gandhiji did not like this idea. Therefore, being much closer to Gandhiji, Lohia could not oppose him. However, Subhash Chander was growing more and more popular everyday and that is why he was elected President of the Congress in 1939.

An agitation of the labourers was going on in Kanpur. The police resorted to fire to control that agitation. Lohia criticized Mr. G.B. Pant who was the Chief Minister of U.P. at that time and due to that reason, Pantji got annoyed with Mr. Lohia.

Inspite of the opposition of Gandhiji, Subhash Chander was elected as President of the Congress. It happened for the first time that a President was elected without the consent of Gandhiji, as Gandhiji had blessed Sita Ramayia Ji for the Presidentship. Gandhiji considered it his own defeat. Later on, it was found out that Subhash Chander was elected because of the support of the socialist group. Though Lohia also liked Subhash Chander Bose but it was a big matter for him to decide as Gandhiji was at one side and socialist group was on the other. Therefore, he decided to remain away from the election of the President. Afterwards, on March 9, 1939 another session of the Congress was held at Tripura, where Govind Vallabh Pant put a resolution that as Gandhiji was our respected national leader so Congress would continue to take guidance from him. Ram Manohar also made a statement in his favour where the dual leadership was suggested. Subhash Chander Bose never liked the interference in his functioning. He did not nominate Nehruji as a member of the executive. As a result, a controversy took place in the Congress leadership. Ultimately, Subhash Chander Bose resigned from the office of the President.

War had broken out in Europe, Gandhiji and others did not want that India should be dragged into this war. At that time, Ram Manohar put a resolution wherein the proposals such as ban on the recruitment from India, refusal to pay the war expenses as well as debt for the war and forming of an organization to oppose the loading and unloading of material for the British ships were passed.

There were two types of views in Congress. One view was that the freedom struggle should be slowed down and the other was that the freedom should be snatched from the Britishers. Ram Manohar Lohia was also in favour of the second view. He made a speech against the Britishers in Calcutta and was arrested immediately after the rally. He was sent to the jail on May 24, but the next day he was released on bail. Later on the case was pursued. Lohia himself defended his case and was ultimately acquitted on August 14.

Dr. Lohia was to leave for Bombay on June 24, to attend a meeting of the Congress Executive. In that meeting he came to know that Pt. Nehru had sent a telegram to the World Peace Council to the effect that if India became free, it would help England. However, Lohia and others criticized this move. In response to that, Jawahar Lal Nehru explained that by support he never meant the military help for the Britishers. So Lohia became silent. Lohia did not like so many views of Nehruji but he never criticized him because both of them were close to Gandhiji and he did not want to hurt the feelings of Gandhiji.

The Second World War was gaining momentum day by day. Common people were dying on all the fronts. With the loss of the most precious human lives, the precious property was also being destroyed. The men who were dying on the war belonged to the common families. In the war front there were fathers, sons, brothers and husbands, and they were being killed on both the sides, without any personal grudge or any enemity. Lohia did not like this type of the warfare. He was messiah of peace and advocated peace for human welfare. However, both the groups were making best efforts to win the war.

On September 9, 1939, a meeting was held between Viceroy of India and Gandhiji wherein Gandhiji conveyed his good wishes for England and expressed that he could never think about the destruction of London. However, the radio reports were giving the impression as though Gandhiji was helping the Britishers.

In June issue of *Harijan*, Lohia wrote an article entitled "Satyagraha Truant" (Immediate protest) where an appeal was made to start the protest immediately and he presented four points before the public, those were as follows:

1. All the communities should be free. They should prepare their own constitution based on the adult franchise.
2. There should be no special privilege for any community at any place.

3. Wherever the capital is installed, whether it is on credit or otherwise, that should not belong to an individual but to whole of the country.
4. Whole of the world should be free from armaments.

Gandhiji was not in favour of immediate protest. He called Mr. Lohia in that context and he too became convinced by his arguments.

Lohia had dedicated his life for the cause of a better society, where there should be no dearth of goods and employment. In that society everyone should be given social security, free medical aid, employment, and everyone must be enjoying the human rights. In order to achieve his dream for a welfare state, he was neither afraid of jail nor he could conceal any of his opinions. He was having hatred towards the British Government and he wanted them to leave his country immediately. Therefore, whenever he got the opportunity to speak or to write against the Britishers, he made full use of it. Lohia was again arrested on June 7, 1940. Later on, it was known that he had been arrested for his speech given on May 11. He was kept in a dark cell of the Sultanpur Kotwali and the next day he was paraded for a distance of 3 miles to present him in the court. At that time, he was handcuffed. When the judge enquired whether he needed the services of a lawyer, he responded that he would himself defend his case. In the court, he gave very long arguments and explained that there was no need of the foreign rulers in India. He further said that he was neither against the people of England nor he wanted its destruction but the attitude of England about India and other countries is not good.

Ram Manohar's father got the news of his arrest. He had always been encouraging his son to contribute whole-heartedly for the freedom struggle of the country. However, being a father he sometimes became worried about the hardships being faced by his son and still wanted his son to marry and lead a settled life. Nevertheless, he was happy that his son was being recognized all over India and was contributing a lot for the formation of a welfare society. He always encouraged his son to do the maximum for this cause and at the same time, he made him aware that he would have to face a lot of hardships on that path.

Due to the arrest of Dr. Lohia the sentiments of general masses were hurt. A letter addressed to Gandhiji, was published in *Harijan* wherein it was questioned that at that time when Lohia and other leaders had been arrested under the Safety Act and the police was perpetrating atrocities on the public, why the agitation was not being started under those circumstances? Gandhiji responded that letter the next day. He answered that he was very sad on the arrest of the Congress leaders as well as of Mr. Lohia, whom he loved most.

However, on July 1, 1941, Lohia was awarded two years imprisonment because of making an instigating speech. Lohia was given the "B" class prisoners' status in the jail. The attitude of the jail officials was not proper. He was tortured brutaly but he bore all the torture. He was always handcuffed with heavy chains. In those days, Shri Parshotam Das Tandon, the Speaker of the U.P. Legislative Assembly, became much surprised to see the heavy handcuffs of Mr. Lohia. Ms. Purnima Bannerji wrote a letter to Mr. Jawahar Lal Nehru regarding the atrocities being afflicted to Lohia in Bareilly jail. There were many references about it in the press. Lohia was shifted from Bareilly jail to Dehradun jail. Here again a large number of people came to see him, whosoever went to see him in the jail was harassed by the police later on. When Lohia knew about it, he was deeply hurt that the people had suffered only because of meeting him. He could not tolerate that the people should suffer because of him. He did not care for his own sufferings but the suffering of the others always hurt him. Hence, he sent a message that he would not meet anyone. So many leaders and socialist workers were in jail in those days. Gandhiji was making various statements for the release of the arrested workers. In a conference in Bombay Gandhiji said that Lohia was a brave person. He was against violence. These words of Gandhiji enhanced his status. On the other side, Lohia was spending his time in writing and reading.

At that time, major changes were taking place in the international politics. The influence of England was decreasing in the international politics. Japan had occupied control over Singapore, Malaysia, Thailand, Burma, Indonesia and so many other islands. Japan, an ally of Germany, was destructing the big centres of England in Asia. So many times, it seemed that the rule of British Empire would finish in Asia. At that time, England felt that Japan should not succeed to occupy India. The Indians were already against England, so in order to win the sympathy of the Indian masses, the Government released all the prisoners from the jail. Dr. Lohia was also released but there was no rest in his life. He started arranging the meetings with his partymen and associates and at last made a plan to intensify the struggle for the freedom of India.

On the other side, the British Government invited the Indian leaders for a dialogue. England sent Mr. Johnson to India to mediate with the leaders of India. From Britishers, Mr. Cripps came with a formula that India would be set free after the World War. The larger group of the Congress was satisfied with this condition. However, Lohia did not agree to this proposal. Rather he waited to intensify the struggle. Nevertheless, the other Congress leaders, including Mr. Jawahar Lal Nehru were not in favour of agitation and they wished to help the Britishers. However, because of the arguments given by Dr. Lohia and others, they could not succeed in their move.

Ram Manohar was in the habit of examining all the issues. He was fully aware about the international events and thought about them. He thought over the impact of all the political happenings. He wrote an article "Betrayal Japan or Self Sufficient Britain" in which he explained that Japan is also a danger for India and it was too late that India might secure England or England might secure India and be cautious about the danger of Japan.

Lohia stayed with Gandhiji for a week in the month of April and it gave them an opportunity to understand each other. Gandhiji felt that Lohia was a man of big heart and brain. He was having deep love for the people of his country and he was prepared to make any sacrifice for his fellow citizens. In the issue of April 26, 1942 of *Harijan*, Gandhiji wrote against England and gave a plan to start the "Quit

India Movement". That movement was based on peace and non-cooperation. Later on the leaders of Congress felt that Gandhiji had been influenced by Dr. Lohia.

The Congress session held at Allahabad in the beginning of 1942 wherein Meera Behan put the resolution of "Quit India" as given by Gandhiji. Gandhiji himself was not in that session. However Lohia and some other leaders wanted that that resolution should be accepted *in toto*. On the other hand, Nehruji and others were against that proposal. Rather there were certain people who wanted to help the Britishers. The aruguments of Lohia and others could not be accepted. Later on, a convention of Congress was held at Almora in which a heated discussion took place. In that convention Lohia criticized Mr. Nehru severely and put a resolution for starting the agitation against Britishers. The foreign capital installed in our country should be confiscated. It was also adopted in the resolution that every country of the world should be free and everybody should have the right to stay at any place of his/her liking. In this way, everybody should be a citizen of the world. Views of Lohia were published in the issue of *Harijan*. A delegation of teachers and students met Lohiaji on July 29. Lohia wanted to start the agitation as well as to avail that appropriate situation at the earliest. However, Gandhiji suggested him to postpone it for the time being and wait for some time.

When Congress passed the resolution of "Quit India Movement" on August 8, 1942, Lohia welcome it and in this way, he got closer to Congress. Gandhiji persuaded the people to support that agitation vigorously. He said that the people who had understood the art of living would die to break the chains of slavery. His slogan was "do or die". There was an impression in a section of the Congress that Gandhiji had accepted the views of Dr. Lohia under his influence. Before the dawn of August 9, Gandhiji was arrested and sent to the jail of Poona. Similarly, so many other Congressmen were arrested on the same night and they were too sent to the different jails of the country. However, Lohia escaped his arrest.

On the other side, there was a great resentment among the people against the Britishers and because of those arrests, the resentment had further increased. They accepted the challenge of the Britishers and decided to support the movement with big vigour. Various meetings were held in different cities and villages for the success of that movement. Ram Manohar had gone underground to secure himself from the arrest and at that time, he was making speeches from the underground Radio Station that was being operated by the Congress. In his speeches, he had been explaining the people about the evils of the slavery, the social evils of the Indian society and the establishment of the socialistic pattern of society. The secret radio was making the broadcasts from Bombay and Calcutta. The radio was also making the people aware with the political consciousness and the international situation. The people used to wait for the time of the Lohia's speech impatiently.

On the other side, the resentment of the people had gone so high that while protesting the Government at different places, they damaged the telephone lines, railway tracks and the electric poles, etc. So many times the police had to resort to firing and cane charging. However, the resentment of the public was increasing. The children, the youth, the old men and women, the students, the farmers, the workers, the traders and the government employees and in fact whole of the country had stood against the British rule. However, the Government was increasing its atrocities to curb this movement.

At that time, this movement was within the control of the socialists whose leader was Ram Manohar Lohia. Through his articles and speeches, he was persuading the people to observe absolute non-cooperation and to obstruct the Government work. The other prominent leaders wre Mr. Parshotam Dass Tandon, Mohan Lal Saxena, Sadiq Ali, Achhuta Patvardhan, Kamla Devi Chattopadhyay, etc. At that time, a number of socialist leaders were in jail. There was great resentment amongst the masses throughout the villages and cities of the country as the Government was arresting one or other political leader. There was a big hatred for the Britishers in whole of the country.

When Lohia smelled the possibility of his arrest, he decided to leave Bombay. He wore the pant, coat, just like Europeans, and painted certain black marks on his face. Thus, changing his identity he reached Calcutta from Bombay. Meanwhile, the revolutionaries looted the Post Office of Manik Tala and it was decided to use whole of the money for freedom movement and not to use a single penny for any other purpose. At that time, he was living in a room of a six storeyed building that was situated in the Central Avenue of Calcutta. Whenever he was to make the speech from the radio, it was announced, "Now listen a message for the freedom fighters". This radio was called the "Congress Radio". When Lohia would not have been there then his previously recorded speech was broadcasted. Lohia was called Banthia Sahib in those days.

Police made a large-scale search for arresting Dr. Lohia. Nevertheless, he was not to be found anywhere. He was being searched in every city of every province. Many persons similar to his identity were informed hiding in certain areas and the police immediately made the raid in those areas. However, when it was found out that that person was not Dr. Lohia the police became more frustrated. Whenever Lohia suspected his arrest, he immediately left that place and started staying at another place. In this way, so many times he had a narrow escape. After some time two of his assistants were arrested. Police applied third degree torture measures on them. In spite of that, they did not utter even a single word about Lohia. Meanwhile Lohia wrote an article "Will Do or Die?". He managed to publish this article and to distribute it throughout the country. Through that article, he persuaded the people for achieving their goal and prepared them psychologically for that.

He was doing very difficult job of publishing so many pamphlets and articles and distributing them. In this period, he wrote a book named "*Jangju Agge Bharo*" (The warrior go ahead) and that book became very popular. Some of its articles were "I am free", "Gandhi" etc. This is our goal and be prepared for revolution. In this way, while leading the revolutionaries he wrote, "The trained and determined, squad of five may be prepared in this way, that as this revolution grows, they may lead the public by going ahead, where there are such squads, there will be beginning of the revolution and the British rule will be finished with a whistle".

Lohia's Arrest in Nepal

This secret radio of the revolutionaries continued its functioning until November 14, 1942. The police was desperately searching Lohia and in November he escaped from the arrest very narrowly. There was a deep concern over his imminent arrest. Therefore, on the suggestion of his well-wishers Dr. Lohia went to Nepal with N.P. Nyman. At the time of his absconding from Hazari Bagh jail, Jaya Prakash Narayan was also staying there. He came to know that many revolutionaries and freedom fighters were hiding in Nepal. How could Ram Manohar rest when his dream was still unrealized? In Nepal, he started working for a group known as "Azad Dasta" (Freedom Squad) engaged in awakening the people about the evils of slavery. The office of this organization was situated on a hilltop known as Bakro or Tapu at Kachhro near the river "Kosi". This office was located only in three huts made up of grass and straw. Nobody knew that activities were going on within those huts for the freedom of India. Ram Manohar Lohia made an effort to install a radio station, but he could not succeed. In Nepal, Jaya Prakash Narayan was living as a Bengali landlord and sister of Achhuta Patwardan was living with him as his daughter.

Indian Government was aware that a number of revolutionaries had taken shelter in Nepal. Nepal became a great rendezvous of freedom fighters. So it was pressing hard for their arrest and expatriation to India. When the revolutionaries got the information that the Nepalese Government had been informed about their hiding place, they immediately decided to shift their office. Those revolutionaries had no source of income nor were they doing any job. Therefore, they were short of money. On the other side, their monetary demands ranging from the expenditure for their meals to the expenditure for purchase of necessary things required for ousting of the Britishers from India demanded a lot of money. Therefore, they sent some of their associates to Calcutta and Patna for bringing money. However, nobody was sure that they would secure themselves from the police. They were immediately arrested in India and on the basis of information given by them. Lohia and Jaya Prakash Narayan were arrested. Suraj Narain who was the Chief of "Azad Dasta", got to know of this.

On the next day when he was brought in the court at Hanumangarh, Ram Manohar Lohia himself defended his case. He pleaded that "he and his friend Jaya Prakash Narayan had come to Nepal as tourists. He further said, "Nepal has been friendly and it is a free country. Nepal has been so friendly to us that it was persuading the Indians to achieve their freedom. Hence, we have committed no crime". However, the Government of Nepal was under the pressure of the British Government and it did not consider the arguments of the defence. For authenticating their identification, some people were summoned from India. Afterwards they were sent to jail.

The Chief of the "Azad Dasta" was making plans to get them free from jail and with this objective he attacked the jail with a number of associates carrying lethal weapons. At first they disconnected the telephone wires and set the huts of the jail guards, situated near jail, on fire. They also put off the lightening gas of the jail and started uninterrupted firing. Instead of facing the challenge, the jail guards fled away. After listening to the gunfires, Jaya Prakash Narayan got up but Lohia kept sleeping. Suraj Narain awoke Lohia made him stand. It was a pitch dark atmosphere so Lohia had to fumble for locating his spectacles. In the deep dark, Jaya Prakash Narayan and his associates came out of jail and due to darkness they got separated from each other. However, they continued to walk towards the pre-decided destination through different passages and they again met on the way. Meanwhile, Lohia's foot was hurt badly and he was feeling much difficulty in walking. However, he continued to walk bearing boldly the severe pain of his foot. On the way, a barbed wire on the way also hurt Jaya Prakash Narayan's foot and it became hard for him to walk. A young man lifted him. In this way, they covered a long distance during the night, crossing crops, fields, stony path and flowing water.

After walking for a long time, they were dead tired and were almost exhausted. It was not possible for them to walk any further but it was very safe for them to go far away from the jail. Hence, they continued to walk although all of them were limping. A marriage party was going on the way and the bridegroom was sitting on the horse. Lohia caught hold of the horse and sat on it. The marriage party thought them to be dacoits and they started running here and there. However, they were made to understand their circumstances, after some time their horse was returned. On the way they also took rest in a house. The next day, when they were passing along, some people were discussing that last night, the dacoits attacked the jail and a number of revolutionaries had been released. They thought that by now that news would have spread up throughout the country and Indian Government must have been informed about the same. Therefore, they wanted to reach a safer place at the earliest for making them fully secured.

They changed their identity according to their personalities. Dr. Lohia put off his spectacles and ruffled his hair. They started to walk further. The wounds of their feet became suppurated and they were bleeding. After some time a river came on their way. They crossed the river on a boat. Nevertheless, the boatman informed the police about their crossing the river. Police followed them but could not find them. As they were disguised in different ways, they safely came at the road of Sialdah Dinazpur.

Lohia in India Again

However, here also they were not feeling themselves secure. They had to be separated for performing different duties and at the same time they had to escape from the police. They were in dire need of money to finance their organization. Amidst that uncertain and disturbed situation, Lohia reached Calcutta and he expected that his old friends would welcome him and would offer him to stay in their houses. To the contrary, he found out that his friends flatly refused to accommodate him on one pretext or the other. On the other hand, Dr. Lohia was having a different type of nature and he had no tendency to put anyone in trouble because of his self-interest. As soon as he discerned that his friends were making excuses, he immediately begged their pardon and went away. He was very uncertain about the place of his stay and had to pass the time by living at different places. He engaged in the activities of the freedom struggle and social welfare. After completion of any task, he became so pleased, that his feelings could not be expressed in words. Whenever he found pessimistic thinking in the public, he got worried. At that time, it was his keen desire that the optimistic feelings and vigour must be created among the public. He decided to see Mr. Subhash Chander Bose in Assam. He reached Assam after changing his identity. But because of less acquaintance, strict vigilance of the army and lack of money, he got entangled in the number of problems. He was not able to meet Subhash Chander Bose and ultimately came back.

Lohia was leading a very hard life in those days. So many times, he had to sleep without food. He had to change his whereabouts every night and it was a very frustrating task. A number of people of his acquaintance were avoiding him, but he was happy that in that freedom struggle he was performing his duties without caring for hunger and thirst. For achieving his goal, he had to go on miles on foot, however, he enjoyed a strange bliss. On the other side, all the police was under the pressure to arrest him. Repeatedly a number of officers were abused for their failure to arrest Lohia and so many were transferred or suspended for their negligence. At one night 11 places were raided simultaneously in Bombay for arresting Lohia but he had a narrow escape. One day police got the correct information of his hideout. But prior to the police raid Dr. Lohia put on suit, necktie, artificial moustaches and made certain black spots on his face. Thus, evading his arrest, he reached Bombay. Later on, he got the news that police reached there, just after his leaving that place.

In Bombay, Lohia went on changing his place of stay by disguising himself. Time and again a number of news items were published in the papers about Dr. Lohia. Though many people had never seen Lohia yet they had deep sympathies for him and had keen interest in the news concerned with him. Dr. Lohia continued his propaganda against British Empire through pamphlets and papers. At that time the British Empire, was ruling over larger area of the earth and the sun never set in their empire. It was also considered the biggest power of that time. Though he was all alone, continuing with his mission, yet he was always in high spirits and always optimistic. At that time, it was the keen desire of everybody to see the photograph and to have maximum information about Lohia. He was becoming a hero of the masses. His popularity was growing to the extent that even in the ordinary meetings, the villagers, the young and old were telling different real or fabricated stories of his bravery.

Lohia's Arrest

It was on May 20, that he was sleeping in a small house on the Babul Nath Road. It was a part of a big building. Police had seized whole of the building from all sides with a very heavy force. Lohia realized that he was helpless. He thought that now it is useless to try to escape and police arrested him. The news of his arrest broke out like a wild fire. When the police officers were taking him away, the people thronged at both sides of the streets, on the roofs of the houses and outside their shops. They were astonished to know that thin man with spectacles was Lohia about whom they had been listening for the last so many years and from whom the British Government was facing the threat. On the next day, the arrest of Lohia was the headline in all the newspapers of India and England.

In those days, the British Government was having two torture centres in India, viz., Nancy Camp and the Fort of Lahore. After bringing to the Fort of Lahore, he was put in a very dark cell. Later on Lohia was inhumanely tortured by the police in the lock up. The Government had trained some persons especially for this purpose. He was kept standing for hours and was not allowed to sleep. Whenever he tried to sleep he was forcibly made to awake. He was handcuffed and shackled. He was tortured as such for ten days. Whenever his eyes closed even for a moment a big cane was struck on the table that created a thumping noise making him awake. He was made to stand up for hours before the officer. One day that officer started abusing Lohia. Lohia kept mum but when he started abusing all the national leaders then Lohia shouted loudly "Shut up your mouth". The officer gave him a very dreadfull look and went away from the room.

Lohia thought that he would bring some gunmen with him and they would again torture him. However, he was prepared for every type of torture. But it did not happen that way. At that night, he was not allowed to sleep even for a moment. Whenever his eyes closed, a big iron cane was struck on the table. On that day, Lohia was feeling fever in spite of that he was made to stand near the wall by some gunmen. Lohia saw towards him and shouted "The Coward of the Fort". Hearing these words that officer and a number of gunmen pounced at him. He was caught from legs and arms and they continued to drag him on the floor for one hour, as a result the gunmen became tired. Lohia was running in fever and his arms and hands were bleeding. He was prepared to face any type of torture. Again he was not allowed to sleep and he was tortured by different ways in the fort.

Chief Officer of the fort became convinced that he would not utter a word in spite of whatever means of torture might be used on him. Then he suddenly changed his behaviour. One day he asked Lohia to sit beside him and all of a sudden started praising him. He said something against the Britishers and wanted to say something about the history of India. However, Lohia took no interest in whatever he said. That officer was very cunning. He touched his feet and made him believe that in fact he had sympathy for him. But Lohia never accepted his hypocritical activities and repeatedly disclosed him the mean activities which were being committed in that fort. One day a hen was taken out of a bag and was hanged upside down before him. It cried and fluttered for a very long time and died. Such types of mean activities were done in his presence just only to hurt his psychological feelings.

After some time Lohia observed that some junior officers and guards had sympathies for him but they were helpless. A guard was so lenient that he provided him all kind of comfort and relief whatever as he could do. But such type of treatment was not expected from any official of the fort towards any prisoner. On the other side, Lohia too never wanted that anybody should suffer because of him. So Lohia declined to accept the sympathies offered by that guard so that he might not be put into any trouble by the senior officers of the fort.

In the Lahore Fort third-degree torturing methods were applied on Dr. Lohia for four months and he was absolutely unaware about outside world. He was never given anything to read nor was he brought outside the fort. As he was forcibly kept awoke for most of the time in jail, so many times he had high fever. He was never given any medicine for fever, however every time he became well at his own. He was kept in the underground dark and dingy cell of the fort. Usually his interrogation started after midnight and irrelevant questions were asked from him. After every interrogation, Dr. Lohia was tortured barbarously and he had become used to that inhuman treatment.

Nobody knew about the whereabouts of Dr. Lohia. His father was helpless and moved from pillar to post to know about the whereabouts of his son, as he wanted to get him released. However, he could not know the place of his confinement. No leader was aware about his confinement in the Fort of Lahore. Even Lohia himself did not know about the confinement of anybody else except him. Later on, he came to know that Jaya Prakash Narayan was also confined there and he too was being tortured inhumanly. The people, in general, were worried about Lohia. Only after 5-6 months, the public got the information that Lohia was confined in a dingy cell in the Fort of Lahore. The help of the law was sought. A famous lawyer Palkiwala appealed in the High Court about the illegal confinement of Dr. Lohia and Jaya Prakash Narayan. People were under the impression that they would get some relief because of that *habeas corpus*. Palkiwala was arrested. It created a big disturbance in the field of law and Government was very much criticized for this action.

All the lawyers of the country condemned this move and the Government was criticized at the international level also. Then the leader of the Socialist Party Ms. Purnima Banerji along with a famous lawyer of Lahore High Court Mr. Jeewan Lal Kapur applied the Second *habeas corpus*. But the Government took a very mischievous turn. It is said that according to the law of 1918 of the Government of India, Lohia and Jaya Prakash Narayan were the state prisoners and *habeas corpus* was not possible for such a crime. Hence, the appeal was withdrawn and after a few days they were made security prisoners. By that time, there was a big news published in the major newspapers about the torture of Lohia for six months. Such news were appearing in all the countries particularly in India and England. It was illegal that no trial was held for such a long time. Ultimately, the Government charged Lohia with sedition, war against the state, murders, etc., and the trial was started. Many lawyers from India and England offered to defend him free of cost. With the growing public pressure and because of the pressure of the Labour Party in England, Lohia was provided some facilities in the jail. At that time, the Labour Party of England also volunteered to send some lawyers to defend him in this case. Now he could see one or two of his lawyers. He was permitted to see some other people also. Lohia made a demand that he should be given some material for reading and writing and his demand was accepted.

Lohia wrote a long letter to the President of the Labour Party of England wherein he mentioned the modern methods of torturing the prisoners, the police attitude towards prisoners and the false cases imposed on him. He also stated that the Government had charged him to be a socialist and the socialists were instigating the violence. He wrote that he did not want to be released but he further stated that there was no person in England who might state that the Secretary of State for Indian Affairs was telling a lie. When he was not given a chance to explain his case, he disclosed the conditions of the people living in a slave country.

Somehow, he sent this letter outside the jail. He wrote to Prof. Laski who had sympathies for the socialists in England. The letter was published in the newspapers of India and England. Because of that, political activities re-started in India and there was resentment amongst the people of India. Regarding his torture, Lohia wrote, "Every Indian knows about *yoga* and *hathyoga*. Such divine experiments are made with human dead bodies or with skull in the graveyard. I feel that with great compulsion I am making the experiments of *hathyoga* under pressure. The physical pain has made my heart and brain equally painful. There are different kinds of this pain. Different pains effect at different times. The pains of the torture go on increasing and the imagination of future pain becomes intolerable. I am related to my thinking only. There should be some limit of my torture. Should I consider the length of the period of my torture as illegal? It may be the decision of the nature that I should remain confined in this torture house till the end of my life".

When the public became aware about the torture of Lohia, Jaya Prakash and other political leaders, letters and articles started to be published daily in the newspapers. The Government's attitude was criticized by the different sections of the society. But Mr. Arthur, the British Secretary denied all the allegations of Lohia. He also tried his best that the allegations made by Lohia should not be published anywhere. In this context, the Government warned the newspapers repeatedly of dire consequences. In jail, after having the facility of writing and reading Lohia remained busy most of the time. Although Dr. Lohia forgot all the torture meted out to him, yet he regretted that if he could be out of the jail he would have contributed a lot for the freedom struggle.

At that time, the thinking of Lohia was not confined only to the Indians. Rather he also thought of every citizen of every slave country where the people were being denied their fundamental rights. Sometimes he thought about the people who were kept in jail without any charge and no trial had started in their cases. He was pained to think about the people who had died because of hunger. At other time, he used to think about the people who died only due to shortage of money for their treatment. Sometimes his heart also panged to think about the children who were compelled to work in hotels, *dhabas*, kilns and factories at a very tender age when they were supposed to play and study in the schools. Their parents had to engage them on such jobs where they had to work day and night, in rain and sunshine, just to fulfil the needs of their families. The flight of his imagination also used to think about the people who were having no shelter, no clothing and no food. Not only this he also thought "that freedom did not mean only to flush out Britishers from India but freedom should be termed as "Complete Economic Security" of everyone. Therefore, maximum efforts should be made for the economic security. . . ."

At the end of 1944, Lohia made another *habeas corpus* and the High Court started hearing of this case. However, an ordinance was issued that the proceedings of the court would not be published. The judge who was hearing them felt that if Dr. Lohia and Jaya Prakash were kept in Lahore jail they could be tortured again. Both of them were transferred to Agra Jail. Hence, both of them were transferred to Agra, and the *habeas corpus* of them got automatically rejected.

There was no difference in their living conditions after their transfer from Lahore jail to Agra jail—same food, same restrictions, same crude and harsh behaviour of the jail authorities. There again Lohia did not felt anything better than reading and writing. His views were published in the newspapers. Further efforts were made for their release. The news about their condition was published in the newspapers of England and discussions about them were held in the British Parliament also. Therefore, a delegation of the British Parliament came to India to see Dr. Lohia and Jaya Prakash Narayan.

It was late of evening and the darkness was spreading. The jail officials were worried because of the visit of that delegation. When they came to the jail, Dr. Lohia and Jaya Prakash Narayan were brought to them escorted by the large number of guards. Rognald Sorson led the delegation and the team remained there for about two hours. On account of the high walls of the jail, the darkness was more intense. Big lanterns were lit to break the darkness but those lanterns were not providing sufficient light. The members of that delegation put so many questions to Lohia and their anxiety to know more about Dr. Lohia was increasing. Then they went to the cell where these prisoners were confined. In the cell they saw some luggage of Lohia but there were a number of books on sociology, philosophy, humanity and poetry. The delegation tried to gather sufficient information about the prisoners and later they were sent back with pleasure. Afterwards the members of the delegation expressed their views that had they moved a little from their belief and principles, they would have been released much earlier. They further said that both Lohia and Jaya Prakash would never do so.

The Second World War ended in 1945. The world saw the biggest destruction. England was no longer a big power and had been rendered much weaker. Gandhiji was released by the end of 1944, later on, the cases of the other prisoners were discussed, and they were released. By the end of 1945, all the prisoners had been released. However, Dr. Lohia, Jaya Prakash Narayan and others who were charged for treason, robbery, etc., were still in the jails and facing their trials. Gandhiji was much worried about the case of Dr. Lohia and his prolonged confinement in jail. Lohia had become used to the jail atmosphere and had no hope of his early release. He used to read and write as usual while sitting in the jail. He was worried for the social, economic and political conditions of his country. Sometimes, he suffered from nostalgia, lost in the memories of village, school, with his friends, grandmother and aunt, and respected father Shri Hira Lal who put him on that path for the welfare of his people. He remembered that his father had created in him the initial awareness about political life. He had a great respect for his father and sometimes used to think that he could not provide him any help and comfort in his old age. He was overwhelmed to think about the sacrifices and the troubles his father had faced for his lovely son.

By that time, his father Shri Hira Lal had become very weak. However, once he came in the jail to see and know the welfare of his beloved son. He put his affectionate hand on the head of Ram Manohar and blessed that he would certainly succeed in his mission. Dr. Lohia asked his father about his family, his village and particularly about the economic conditions of the village. However, the time of meeting in jail was limited. While returning from the jail his father again put his hand affectionately on his head and said it would be difficult for him to visit there again. Ram Manohar stood there for a long time looking the back of his father and ultimately bowed his head towards him. He came back to his cell with heavy heart and that was really the last meeting of the father and the son. After a few days his father expired.

When Ram Manohar got the news about the death of his father, he bore that irreparable loss with courage and paid homage to his father by closing his eyes. He bowed his head while paying regards to his dear father. In spite of this tragedy, the Government did not allow him to see his family members. So many inmates of the jail expressed their sympathies to him and he thanked them all. Some people suggested him to go out on parole but he did not accept because that facility was not provided to everyone.

Afterwards, Dr. Lohia came to know that when his father was going to attend a meeting by bus he had a heart attack on the way and died on the spot. Ram Manohar reminisced that his father had continuously struggled for the freedom of the country and was a strong opponent of the Britishers. He used the terms 'dishonest', 'cruel', 'aggressors' 'cheats' 'hypocrites', etc., for the Britishers for which he had to face jail-term in 1929, 30 and 40 on account of taking part in the freedom struggle. Once Hira Lal went to participate in a big Conference of the Congress held at Delhi in 1941 on foot. It was the month of summer; the temperature was very high. Carrying the flag of Congress he was leading the procession. On the way the police resorted to lathi charge. Police tried to snatch the flag from Hira Lal but he did not lose hold of it.

Shri Hira Lal was also fond of reading. He had approximately 600 books on different subjects in his house. He took active part in all the freedom movements launched by the Congress. He was the admirer of Gandhism and always resorted to propagate against the British Government.

The elections were held in England. The Labour Party was much popular in those days. It secured the absolute majority. They were in favour of granting freedom to India. Government started dialogue with Congress and other parties. Gandhiji put a condition to the effect that Dr. Lohia and Jaya Prakash Narayan should be released unconditionally so that congenial atmosphere might be created. The year of 1945 ended and the year of 1946 ushered in. At that time, all the people, legal experts, Congressmen, Gandhiji and other leaders were trying their best for acquitting them from all the charges.

Out of Jail

On account of strong pressure of the public on one side and lack of adequate proofs available with the prosecution on the other side, the Government ordered for the withdrawal of all the cases against Lohia and ultimately it was declared that he would be released on April 11, 1946. In the morning of April 11, people from many parts of the country started gathering in front of the gate of Agra jail to welcome him. So many people had not seen Lohia earlier and most of them had not seen even his photograph. However, they had listened much about him. Therefore, thousands of people gathered before the jail gate to welcome him. They waited for a long time and sun had set. There was uncertainty that he would be released today or not. However, in the evening, when the gate of the jail was opened, Jaya Prakash Narayan and Lohia wearing the white khaddar and Gandhi cap came out of the jail. They were having some luggage and there were certain bags filled with books. Those books had been Lohia's good friends in the jail. There was smile on their faces. As soon as they were released from the jail, the people raised sky rending slogans, i.e., "Ram Manohar Lohia Zindabad" and "Jaya

Prakash Narayan zindabad". Both of them were loaded with garlands. People lifted them on their shoulders and a large number of people touched their feet.

That huge gathering turned into a procession and the local leaders were worried about their security. Lohia stood on an open jeep and that procession began to proceed towards the city. To celebrate the occasion in a befitting manner, the people threw flowers, garlands and they were served water, *sharbat* and the *laddoos* on the way. Women were standing on the roofs of the houses. They were paying obeisance to Dr. Lohia and Jaya Prakash Narayan from the roofs. Some of the women were performing *aarti* for their long lives. Both of the leaders were smiling at that time. As they were free after four years' confinement, they were much sensitive at that time and were unable to utter anything.

On the same night, Lohia proceeded to Calcutta. On the way, he was thinking about his father as he had put him on the path of freedom struggle. Dr. Lohia thought that feelings of his father must have been hurt because of the sufferings he had to face in the jail. However, he came to jail where he blessed him and prayed for his success in his mission. He was overwhelmed to think that his father was very simple, honest and hard worker and above all he had sympathies and love for the general masses. He was paying his respect to that great soul from his heart. So many times, he became deeply sad on the thought that he had been deprived of an ideal father.

He did not waste any more time. He met his friends at Calcutta. Contrary to his last experience, his friends welcomed him this time but Lohia felt that they were still under fear. He again started writing articles and arranged certain meetings. After a week he got a message from Delhi to attend a meeting of the Congress executive as a special invitee. He also got a message from Gandhiji to see him as he could not see Gandhiji after his release from jail. Aruna Asif Ali also sent him the message for the same purpose. He too wanted to know the views of Gandhiji and other leaders so he came to Delhi.

Meanwhile the Government of the Labour Party had been formed in England. They wanted to free India and for this purpose Mr. Attlee, the Prime Minister of England sent a delegation of three cabinet ministers to India. This delegation was termed as Cabinet Mission. The members of delegation also invited the Muslim League as a separate party. Muslim League was demanding a separate homeland for Muslims by division of India. Lohia was totally against this demand. Therefore, Lohia visited different parts of the country and made the people aware of the weaknesses of the Cabinet Mission. By arranging meeting at different places, he informed the party workers, the students that the British Government was bowing down under pressure, and they should continue their freedom struggle. Wherever Lohia had gone, he was given a warm welcome and his views were also corroborated.

Goa Struggle

Lohia's health was deteriorating day-by-day. He was advised complete rest but due to rush of daily routine work he had to work till late night. Meanwhile, he got a message from his aunt (wife of the elder brother of his father) to the effect that she was ill and wanted to meet him immediately but due to business and pre-engagements, he could not go to meet her. However, on 6th May he came to Mirzapur to meet her aunt unexpectedly. When the people of Mirzapur came to know about his arrival, they arranged a grand function for his welcome where many leaders welcomed him.

Lohia had a very affectionate friend, Mr. Julius Messeng in Goa. He had invited Lohia so many times to visit Goa. Lohia thought it would be proper to visit Goa and stay there for some days for his physical and mental rest. He was also advised by the doctors to do so. He went to Goa on June 10, 1946, where he observed that Goa had been under the Portuguese control for the last 500 years and the conditions at that place were similar to that of India. In Goa people were denied human rights to the extent that even for printing an invitation card, the permission was taken from the Government. When he thoroughly studied the situation, his feelings were greatly hurt to know that the people of Goa had not made any attempt or launched any movement for their freedom. When the people of Goa came to know that Lohia had come over there, they came to see him. Mr. Parshotam Kakodkar, who was single-handedly struggling for freedom, also came to see Dr. Lohia. He arranged a public rally in Panjim on June 15 after making consultation with Lohia. Mr. Parshotam sent about 200 invitation cards to the people who wanted to free their beloved country from the Portuguese.

A large number of people took part in that rally. Lohia spoke for about an hour and inspired the people to start the freedom struggle. Accordingly, it was resolved that from June 18 the movement for freedom would be launched. A meeting will be held at Madhgav Ded Modar Vidya Bhawan for the success of that movement. However, the Government received the information about the proposed meeting and it became very confused. In that meeting it was suggested by some people that the movement should be postponed for six months for making appropriate arrangements. Nevertheless, both Dr. Lohia and Kakodakar stressed that the meeting itself had been called for making arrangements.

On June 18, thousands of people reached Madhgav, from where the freedom movement was to be launched. They were raising sky-rendering slogans of "Dr. Lohia Zindabad" and "Mahatma Gandhi Zindabad". Although it was a huge gathering, yet the police had arranged to control it. At about 4.15 p.m., Dr. Lohia accompanied by his friend

Julis Meisseng came to that place on a horse-driven vehicle. After getting down from the vehicle when they started to go towards the stage, the administrator of the city ordered Lohia to go back. In spite of that, Lohia did not stop and continued to proceed. The slogans of Lohia Zindabad were being continuously raised by the people. They also welcomed him with garlands. The army men and police guards armed with guns and firearms had surrounded the place. As soon as Lohia started to speak, the administrator pointed his pistol at him and it seemed that he would fire. Suddenly an atmosphere of panic and uncertainty prevailed there but Lohia went ahead with courage. He caught hold the administrator's hand and said, "Be patient. Do you not see that a large number of people are here? It would result into mass bloodshed. Do you want to maintain peace or not?" The administrator became helpless. It was the first time that the people saw the administrator had to bow before non-violence and they were very pleased. Later on police arrested Dr. Lohia and his friend Julius Meisseng and they went silently along with them, as they did not want any bloodshed.

After that, the stage secretary started reading the written speech of Dr. Lohia as follows:

> "I do not care for the Government of Portugal. The tyranny of Portugal will end ultimately. It will be the first step to remove the infamous laws that are against the human rights. Goa is a part of Hindustan and I am a Hindustani so every Hindustani must help the Goan people".

It was the first time that the Goan people had learnt the lesson of non-violence and they got the lesson that they could express their resentment with peaceful means adopting the path of non-violence.

On the next day all these events and the speech of Dr. Lohia were published in the leading newspapers of India. People appreciated the courage and sobriety of Dr. Lohia and his concern for the people of Goa. After that, the freedom struggle of Goa was linked with the freedom movement of India and Indians raised the voice that Goa, being a part of India, should also be freed simultaneously.

Lohia and his friend were brought to the police station but there was a feeling of resentment among the people. So they reached at the police station in the form of a procession. The police had to resort to lathi-charge to disperse the crowd. However, they did not move even after bearing the blows of lathis and they continued to raise slogans of "Lohia Zindabad." After making all efforts, the Police Chief could not be able to disperse the crowd. At last, he came to Lohia and asked him to request the people to go away. As Lohia never wanted that anybody should suffer because of him, he came out and requested the people to go away. At that instant, the people started to disperse. At that time, it was raining heavily but the people did not bother about the rain. After looking that scene, Lohia became sure that the people of Goa were prepared to fight and struggle for the freedom and this struggle would continue.

Lohia was kept in a dark and dingy cell in the jail. There was no provision of any bathroom or toilet. At that time, a rumour went on floating that the people were preparing to attack the Madhgav jail for setting Lohia free from it. Because of these rumours, Lohia was transferred to the Panjim jail. The place, from where Lohia was arrested, was near the Office of the Municipal Committee. The people named that crossing as "Lohia Chowk". Ram Manohar Lohia and his friend were to be released from the jail on June 19 and the people in thousands gathered there to receive them. They were raising slogans in favour of Lohia and against the Government. After seeing the continuous increase of the gathering, the administrator came to Lohia and again asked him to request the people to disperse. However, Lohia did not agree to it. Police resorted to lathi charge to disperse them but the crowd did not move. Meanwhile, the Government of Goa issued orders for sending Lohia away across the border of Goa in the territory of India. When police was taking Lohia away from the Goan territory, he shouted, "If the civil liberties are not granted to the people within three months, he will come again and will re-start the movement." The police brought Lohia at the Komail Border and released him at the Border of India.

When the people came to know that Lohia had been deported to India, they attacked the Panjim Police Station. Consequently, they decided to hold a conference on June 27 at the "Lohia Chowk". The Goan Government was so frightened that it tried to gain the sympathy of the leaders of the freedom movement and passed an order that there was no need to seek any permission for holding a general rally.

It was an irony that Lohia had visited Goa to take rest but to the contrary he became more busy than earlier. Many leaders of India appreciated Lohia's activities in Goa. In the 26 June issue of the *Harijan* it was mentioned that, "From the last 188 years, the Goans were deprived of the human right of forming any association or organization. . . . Lohia has broken this law and he has served the cause of providing civil liberties to the people of Goa ". . . . Now I can say to the Goan people not to be afraid of the Portuguese Government".

At that time, many leaders were not in favour of linking Goa's freedom with the freedom of India. Jaya Prakash Narayan and Patel were also of the same view. Nehru was also having the same opinion. He made a speech in Bombay on July 10 where he said that there was no need of movement against the Government of Goa because with the end of British Power, Portuguese power would finish automatically. Only Gandhiji supported Dr. Lohia's move to link the movement of Goan freedom with the India's struggle for freedom. On July 12 Lohia made a statement, i.e., "The emotional people of Goa stood bravely against the cruel law. . . We are also having the support of Gandhiji." So many people were not aware about the problems of Goan people and they got the knowledge about the need of freedom of Goa through the activities of Dr. Lohia. A big rally was held at Bombay where Lohia's work was appreciated and he was presented with a bag of Rs. 15,000.

Where because of only one visit of Lohia the people of Goa became aware about their rights and launched a freedom movement, there the Goan Government was much frightened and to suppress this movement it began to adopt administrative as well as political measures. In this reference Gandhiji received a letter from the Governor of Goa on July 18, which read, "You are unnecessarily intervening with the affairs of Goa. . . Only unsatisfied people have joined this movement. . . The civil liberties of Goa are not in danger".

In response to that Gandhiji published a letter in the August 14 issue of *Harijan* to this effect, "I cannot agree with your argument that this movement is limited only to a few unsatisfied people. . . . The eight years' confinement of Dr. Bandhaja by your Martial Law is a sufficient proof of the civil liberties available in Goa. . . You as well as the citizens of Goa should congratulate Lohia lightening this lamp. . . . Actually the Portuguese who have come from Portugal are different. . . I hope that you would rethink for your pro-public liberties and your own views".

After the release of Lohia he was offered the Office of the Secretary of the Congress Party but he rejected this offer very politely. He was having his different views about the organization of the party. He was of the view that no member of the executive of the party should become President, Prime Minister or the Minister either in Central or in the State Government. The socialist group in the party was of the view that this path should be adopted. Lohia was of the opinion that the political leaders should serve the public without cherishing any objective to gain power. Moreover, they should advise the government to take every step for the welfare of the public. This socialist group was of the opinion that the socialistic pattern of society should be established after the independence of the country. By doing so there would be equality of wealth and equal social and political rights would be available to everyone and special reservations would be given to the backward classes with a view to bring them at par with the upper classes. They suggested that some special efforts should be made for it. Lohia wished that Congress should have a flawless and distinct image.

The party has not emerged as per the views of Dr. Lohia. He never wanted that any party worker should join the Government before Independence. However, Congress believed in forming the Government. Lohia made a statement on August 1, 1946, which read "The party's decision not to join the Constituent Assembly could not be published properly. . . . It is not the Constituent Assembly but the power of the people that is our way".

The other leaders who had similar concept also wanted that members of the executive should not accept the offer to become Ministers. They believed that remaining out of the Government, they could provide better guidance and direction to the Government and they could achieve their adopted goals very easily. The party should expand its base first and attaining power should not be its goal. Lohia was determined with his views that politics should be a means to serve the public. The socialists were fully determined to do the maximum for the welfare of the masses; however, their number was very small.

Gandhiji was a staunch supporter of Dr. Lohia. He was in favour of launching of freedom struggle in Goa. On September 21, i.e., after three months from his arrival from

Goa he met Gandhiji and discussed the affairs of Goa. He addressed a meeting of the Goans at Bombay. The Goan Government got this information and they banned his entry in Goa. The Indians as well as Goans also suggested Lohia not to visit Goa because they feared that Lohia might be sent to jail, which might cause an obstacle for his useful contribution for the freedom struggle. Thus, his useful time would be wasted in jail. Nevertheless, Lohia was not willing to accept it and he said, "I have promised. . . I cannot stop". Before leaving for Goa he addressed various meetings and rallies at different places such as Poona, Sagli Mirza etc. He reached Belgav on September 29. When he reached at Komail in Goa, the police arrested him. He was confined in the fort of Arabad on that night. The conditions of that fort were very uncongenial. The diet was very poor. There was no provision of bathroom or toilet. The prisoners were not allowed to come out from the cell or meet with the outsiders. There was no provision for reading or writing. On the other side, Gandhiji was pressurizing the Goan Government for the release of Lohia. The people of Goa were also preparing to launch a movement for the release of Lohia and for this purpose, they arranged meetings at different places.

By that time, an interim government had been formed in India. On his birthday, i.e., October 2, Gandhiji wrote a letter to the Viceroy of India to seek the release of Lohia from Goa and in response to that the Viceroy of India and the priest of Portugal made efforts and Lohia was brought through Janmodh and was released in the territory of India. On October 8, a restriction of 5 years was imposed on the entry of Lohia. In the territory of India near the Goan border Lohia visited different places from October 28. Lohia wrote a letter to the Judge of Goa wherein he wrote "I have not broken a single law of Goa. . . The Government of Goa should seek apology from me and should pay the compensation for my illegal confinement". Gandhiji published this letter in *Harijan* and also gave his comments which read, "It is not an ordinary letter. Dr. Lohia is not a common man and there is a national Government in India. Come what may, people's mandatory power and the Government would certainly support Dr. Lohia."

Lohia was attending various meetings in the different cities adjoining the border of Goa. All of a sudden he received a message of Gandhiji to visit Delhi. However, when he reached Delhi Gandhiji had left for Noakhali. Therefore, Lohia came back to Belgav and started attending his pre-arranged meetings. Here again he received a telegram from Gandhiji wherein he expressed his desire to see him. Dr. Lohia left for Calcutta and Gandhiji asked him to stay at Noakhali. Here they discussed various issues such as the impending problems of the Government, India's independence and the establishment of socialistic pattern of society in India. They discussed these problems thoroughly. At that time, the Government did not want Lohia to take part in the movement of Goa. Nevertheless, Lohia was of the view that the people of Goa had become aware about their independence and that was the high time to accelerate the freedom struggle for compelling the Portuguese to leave their control over Goa.

Lohia had the feeling that Goa's freedom struggle must

be linked with the independence of India and at that time if the leadership is not provided, the movement would be failed. Hence, he sent a message to them for continuing their movement in a non-violent way. He further advised them to face the lathi blows or bullets without any fear and compell the Europeans to leave Asia. Dr. Lohia had become a popular figure in Goa. The women had added his name in their folk songs and 'Borker' a famous poet of Goa, wrote, "Great Lohia, great is this land and great are its sons". Lohia called a meeting at Jinnah Hall on January 1, 1947 in Bombay with a view to continue their struggle. The majority of the people in this meeting belonged to Goa and he appealed them to collect money for the movement. Thousands of rupees were collected and the women even donated their ornaments.

In the month of January 1947, the British Prime Minister announced the independence of India. Lord Mountbatten was sent as the Viceroy of India in place of Lord Wavel. Lord Mountbatten prepared a scheme to divide India into two parts. Congress accepted this scheme but Lohia and Gandhiji did not accept it and said that the division of India would take place on their dead bodies. The socialists did not want the division of the country.

Lohia called a conference of socialist party in Kanpur from February 26 to 28. In this conference, the word of "Congress" was deleted from the "Congress Socialist Party" and it was renamed as "Socialist Party". Lohia felt that now as the Congress had become a part of the Government, the socialists would have the opportunity to criticize the Congress and to pin-point the mistakes of the Government.

In this connection Lohia said, "To delete the word 'Congress' does not mean the opposition of Congress. . . Congress has become a part of the Cabinet. Now the socialists shall have the opportunity to fight with Congress and some justice will be available".

Decision to Divide the Country

In June 1947, a meeting of Congress High Command was held in Delhi. Gandhiji was not in favour of the division of the country but he was taking the views of the different leaders. At that time, Shri Kirplani was the President of Congress. Lohia was also against the division of the country. However, Nehru and Patel were in an aggressive mood at that time. A controversial and hot discussion was held between Lohia and Patel. Lohia tried his level best to make him understand the two-nation theory and also explained the other dangers connected with that theory. Maulana Azad, Khan Abdul Ghafffar Khan, etc., were also present in that meeting. Gandhiji had realized that the division of the country would certainly take place. He was very much disturbed on this account asked the Assembly to write to the Viceroy that Congress had accepted the method of division but no British authority should remain here to practise it. The representatives of Congress and Muslim League would sit together to practise it.

In the meantime, Lohia went to Calcutta where a delegation of Nepalese met him. They were against the monarchy of Nepal and by that time Lohia had emerged as a progressive leader and well-wisher of the whole mankind. The Nepalis wanted Lohia to lead their movement and for this purpose, they invited Lohia to Nepal. Lohia accepted their invitation and advised them to form a National Level Party. Some of the people suggested naming it as "Nepali Rashtri Congress". After some days, another delegation of Nepalese met Lohia and he was invited to attend a Conference scheduled to be held at "Sokia Pokri" near Darjeeling on April 25. He accepted that invitation also. While he was proceeding Sokia Pokri by a bus to attend this conference, he was stopped on the way and was forbidden to go ahead by the police. Dr. Lohia did not agree and was arrested for the non-compliance of the orders. However, he was released after two hours. He again tried to proceed towards that conference but was restricted by the police. He wanted to stay there for some more time, but he got a message from Delhi. He never wanted to go to Delhi where the leaders were having their eyes on power. However, he was of the view that socialists should not try to attain power. Rather they should serve the people without any self-interest. He also viewed that in independent India, socialists should work for providing economic freedom and equal opportunities for all and sundry. He had no inclination of gaining power or recognition. On receiving message, he reached Delhi. In those days, the violent clashes amongst Hindus and Muslims took place at many places. Nehru, who earlier had love and affection for Dr. Lohia, did not give importance to his views. However, Lohia was very much close to Gandhiji, but Gandhiji could not impress the Congress leaders by the views of Lohia. Therefore, he was a dejected man in those days. Lohia made maximum efforts to check the Hindu-Muslim clashes at many places even by putting his life in danger. At that time, maximum clashes amongst Hindus and Muslims took place in Bengal. Muslim League declared direct action day on 16th of August. Keeping in view this declaration, Lohia was so worried that he immediately made up his mind to visit Bengal and Assam. He directed all his party workers to do whatever was required to check these clashes. Lohia was informed that there is a great danger of Hindu-Muslim riots in Chittagong area. Lohia made a sudden programme to go to Chittagong. But when he reached the railway station to board the train he came to know that the train had already gone. However, some people at the railway station identified him and they decided to send him by goods train. In this way, Dr. Lohia reached Chittagong.

Dr. Lohia arranged a peace conference at Chittagong. But before the beginning of the conference, the District Magistrate appeared there and he inspected the areas all around the place of meeting. However, as soon as the D.M. had gone, miscreants suddenly appeared and attacked those people who were sitting peacefully on their seats. It was the tragic incident in which many innocent people were killed and so many others were injured.

So many people ran away from the conference to save their lives. A few people were left there but Lohia was determined to hold the conference. Alhough there was a deep psychological burden on his mind yet he stayed there for establishing eternal peace. However, keeping in view the danger to his life, the party workers dragged and hidden him in a house. Nevertheless, the goondas followed him and surrounded that house. As party workers had also gathered there in a large number so nobody dared to attack Dr. Lohia. In the next morning, Lohia went to the other places where the clashes were taking place. He was very much aggrieved. Nobody was ready to pay heed to his words. The goonda elements from both sides were not accepting his views from both the sides but he was going ahead without caring for his life. After making maximum efforts for a few days he again returned to Calcutta.

Reaching at Calcutta, he formed a volunteer task force known as "Gan Fauj" to check the clashes. Most of the people in that force were the party workers.

In December 1946, the clashes had taken a very serious turn in Noakhali. Gandhiji was there to create a peaceful atmosphere. Lohia also reached there. They were having two objectives, i.e., to remove the feelings of distrust between Hindus and Muslims and to create the national feelings. Lohia started a relief camp in Kanshipur while a meeting of the Constituent Assembly was going on in Delhi. However, both Gandhiji and Lohia were having no interest in that meeting. Their minds were occupied only to promote Hindu-Muslim unity and cooperation. After a few days, Gandhiji sent Lohia to Calcutta with the instructions to visit the houses of his Muslim friends so that they might jointly work for the Hindu-Muslim unity.

After reaching Calcutta, Lohia prepared a list of his Muslim friends. At first it seemed him very easy to visit the houses of Muslims accompanied by his Muslim friends.

However, after some time he realized that that was a very difficult task. The distrust among the people was so intense that neither the Muslims were willing to go to the houses of the Hindus nor the Hindus were prepared for visiting to the houses of Muslims. Lohia was astonished to work out that what had happened in those few days. Calcutta was divided between Hindus and Muslims. Muslims were afraid of going to the Hindu localities and likewise Hindus considered it dangerous to enter the Muslim localities. None of his Muslim friends was interested in meeting Dr. Lohia on one pretext or the other because they did not want to put Lohia's life in danger.

After analyzing the situation thoroughly, Lohia decided that he would go alone in the Muslim houses. After knowing their feelings, he would try to remove their mistrust and misunderstanding. For that purpose, one day, he decided to visit a Muslim locality. His friends forbade him to do so. However, he did not agree. As soon as he entered into that Muslim locality the Muslims were looking at him suspiciously. Nobody was prepared to have a talk with him. Accompanied by a Muslim child he went to the hostel of the Muslim students. He met with some students. Lohia told them his identity as well as his purpose to meet them. They talked with him hesitatingly.

On the other side, the associates of Lohia were worried about him. About three hours had passed. Lohia talked with them for about two hours and removed their doubts. Lohia said in unequivocal terms that Mr. Jinnah Sahib had committed a big mistake by accepting the idea of division of the country. Those students also very clearly said, "If you consider Jinnah a traitor, we too consider you a traitor . . ." But later on it was concluded that many incidents had taken place on account of mistrust without any basis. The students requested Lohia to come again and assured him that they would do the maximum to promote the Hindu-Muslim Unity. Meanwhile, night had fallen and darkness had spread. So those students accompanied Lohia up to the Hindu localities providing him full security.

Lohia made a statement, "If a Muslim would be killed in the territory of India it would be a sin and irreligious act. Similarly, Government should make it clear to the Pakistan and its founders that if they treat the minorities badly, India will stop to provide them coal, iron, cloth, etc. till they do not improve themselves".

But nobody was paying any heed to such statements and violent clashes had become serious day by day in Calcutta, Noakhali, Patna, Delhi and the different cities of Punjab. It had caused a big loss of lives and property.

On the next day, a meeting of the socialist party was held. Socialists believed that perhaps Gandhiji's viewpoint would be accepted and that might safeguard the destruction of the country. However, the British Government did not accept this plea of Gandhiji. At that time the news about violent clashes amongst Hindus and Muslims at different places were reaching there. Those reports were causing big grief to the socialists. Lohia was of the opinion that Muslims should stay there. He said, "Let the people migrate from Pakistan, but the people from India should not be sent to Pakistan". But there were a number of obstacles to make that scheme practicable. Gandhiji, Lohia, socialists and communists were not in favour of this type of division. However, they were helpless. The country had been divided into Bharat and Pakistan. Punjab and Bengal were divided.

Gandhiji reached Calcutta on August 9. The results of clashes were visible on the way. There was not a single person at the railway station and even the driver of the train was not available. There prevailed an atmosphere of insecurity. Gandhiji decided to go on foot but the volunteers of Gan Fauj reached there and they took the risk to drive the train. The train had not started yet but the Muslim hooligans surrounded it. The volunteers of Gan Fauj raised the slogans of "Hindu-Muslim Unity" and "Hindu Muslim Bhai Bhai" (Hindu Muslim are brothers). As a result of that the atmosphere became calm and this incident was published in the newspapers. This incident also created a very good impact on the people all over the country. This move was fully appreciated and people became active for the Hindu-Muslim Unity.

Independent India

India was going to become an independent country on August 15, 1947 while Pakistan had become a separate country on August 14, 1947. Lohia was invited to attend various functions at Delhi. However, to put a check on the Hindu-Muslim clashes was the main objective of Lohia. Hence, he visited various places accompanied by Gan Fauj for creating a peaceful atmosphere. He was also successful in his mission. In the evening of August 14, Lohia arranged a mass rally at Shardanand Park in Calcutta wherein he paid rich tributes and regards to the people who had suffered or sacrificed their lives for the cause of the freedom.. While addressing the meeting he said, "Today is the last night of slavery than why to sleep". After the rally Lohia led a procession and which was taken out through different bazaars of the city throughout the night in which the slogans of Hindu-Muslim unity were raised. The morning of 15th of August was a different morning for the people. People were congratulating each other.

A number of functions were arranged on 15th August in the city where Lohia was expected to address. However, Lohia thought that the country was facing serious problems and their solution depended upon the leaders of the country. At that time the main problems of the country were hunger, unemployment, inequality, backwardness and denial of human rights. To work on these lines was the main programme for him and his associates. Therefore, while people were participating in different functions, Lohia was making the people aware about the new problems that had emerged in the country.

The clashes between Hindus and Muslims had been subdued after a few days and peace was restored. However, on August 31, these clashes again erupted all of a sudden. Gandhiji went on fast and vowed that he would not take anything till the peace is restored. Lohia formed a "Peace Committee" and gathered all of his associates. He requested the people to surrender their arms and after some days the atmosphere of peace and love again prevailed. Thus, Gandhiji also broke the fast.

Once again the riots took place in Delhi. Gandhiji accompanied by Lohia went to Delhi and started to establish peace but desired success could not be achieved for some days. Refugees in large number were living in Delhi. There was a big task before the government to reinstate them and to arrange for their residences. At that time, a big feeling of mistrust prevailed amongst the Muslims. They were afraid of moving alone in Delhi. They were living in an atmosphere of fear and uncertainty. There was an essential need to restore the feeling of trust and security amongst them. Lohia visited many Muslim houses and arranged meetings for restoring communal harmony. One day when he was going in a car along with a Muslim boy, a crowd on the way stopped him. That crowd asked Lohia to hand them over that boy as they needed his blood. Lohia tried to calm them down but they were not agreed to accept his pleas. Some persons shouted "Who are you? Where were you at that time when Hindus were being murdered"? In response Lohia said, "Most of the time I had been confined in the Lahore fort. When I was bearing torture then where were you"? Lohia was standing between the car and the crowd as a wall. He did not want to hand over that boy. However, the crowd proceeded ahead with a view to snatch the boy from him. However, at that time, a lorry of army appeared there and the crowd asked the army that they were carrying arms. The army forwarded and searched the boy and the car. After making thorough search they asked the crowd that there were no arms in the car and allowed them to go ahead.

During those days Dr. Lohia and Gandhiji received a message from Calcutta that the situation was turning from bad to worst and both of them should visit there at the earliest. Gandhiji sent Lohia on this mission and instructed him to have regular contact with him. The Cabinet of the Congress had been formed by that time and the Ministers were performing the duties in their respective departments. All the Ministers belonged to the Congress party. One day, Lohia appealed to the Minister for Rehabilitation to call a meeting of Hindu-Muslim and Sikhs. The main objective of this meeting was to create communal harmony among them. However, the Minister had been postponing that meeting repeatedly without any reason. Lohia felt that he would not be calling the proposed meeting because he had requested him for the same. Then he sought the permission from Gandhiji that if he deemed fit, the socialist party might call a meeting. Gandhiji felt it proper and permitted Lohia to call the meeting.

Lohia called a huge meeting of Hindus, Muslims and Sikhs in Delhi. The representatives of all the communities attended that meeting. The meeting of the Congress Executive was also to be held on the same day. The meeting called by the socialists started at 12.00 and that of Congress Executive started at 12.30. Gandhiji was sitting in the meeting called by the socialists and he was listening to the views of everyone. However, as the meeting of the Congress started, Gandhiji received various messages to attend their meeting. Gandhiji was satisfied in that meeting and he sent a message that they might continue the meeting without him. Nevertheless, the members of the Executive Committee of Congress kept waiting and they felt that Lohia was responsible for it. The meeting called by socialists continued for three hours and since Gandhiji did not go in the meeting of the Congress Executive, they postponed it. This caused more distance between Nehru and Lohia.

The Socialists were small in number, however, they were very determined. They were determined to make efforts for establishing a socialistic pattern of society with a view to bring prosperity and secure human rights in the country. Lohia had been invited throughout the country with a view to establish the memorials of martyrs and the functions in their memories and he was attending these functions as a moral duty. Lohia neither wanted any office nor wanted to interfere in the functioning of the Government. He had only one objective and that was the Hindu-Muslim unity and the social reforms at that time. He was nominated as a member of the food committee on the recommendation of Gandhiji. The other members of the Committee were Mr. Parshotam Thakur Das, Mr. G.D. Birla, Dr. V.K.R.V. Rao. Dr. Lohia put forward certain suggestions, i.e., growing of more food, putting ban on imports, promotion of cooperation, control on prices and the proper use of the available food. He remained the member of the committee for some time but he was not satisfied with its functioning so he resigned from its membership.

The Congress leaders did not like the closeness between Lohia and Gandhiji. On the other side, Gandhiji liked the views of Lohia and he preferred to keep Lohia with him. A number of times Lohia sought permission from Gandhiji for going outside Delhi but he restricted him. Congress leaders were under the impression that perhaps Lohia wanted to join Government through Gandhiji but that presumption was totally baseless. One day when Dr. Lohia was going to see Gandhiji and Sardar Patel was coming out of Gandhiji's residence. Sardar Patel addressed Lohia in a sarcastic way "Do you want to oust me. . ." Lohia became surprised after listening Patel's remarks. He was not expecting this, from a leader of very high stature. Lohia had to listen such sarcastic remarks from other leaders also. However, he always became sad after listening such remarks because he wanted nothing more than social reforms, economic development and the promotion of human rights. Nevertheless, it was true that he was not happy with the functioning of the Government and he used to criticize the Government. He did so in order to bring about improvements in the functioning of the Government. Once, Sardar Patel made a complaint to Gandhiji to the effect that, according to a C.I.D. report, Lohia wanted to oust the Government of "Aun Suang" of Burma through an underground movement. When Lohia was asked about it he called it a "false allegation". Gandhiji relied on simplicity, truthfulness, honesty and bravery of Lohia. Therefore, he desired to see that report. However, in spite of his repeated demands, the report was not shown to him and later on, it was said that the report had disappeared.

Some more efforts were made to defame Dr. Lohia. A number of allegations were imposed on him. One day a report appeared in newspaper that 303 guns were recovered from a Muslim area, where Lohia had been working for restoration of peace. This news made havoc and there was panic among the public. Lohia examined this report and it was detected that only a single gun of 303 mark had been recovered. However, because of this news, controversy arose and it made adverse effect in his efforts, which were in progress for restoring peace. Gandhiji discussed that report with Dr. Lohia and after thorough discussion Lohia said, "This report made by the Ministry of Information and Broadcasting has spoiled the efforts of many weeks". In response to that Gandhiji said, "Can you run this Ministry? Why are you running away from the responsibility?" During the discussion, Lohia said very seriously, "First you should decide that Congress leaders are not the best in the country, only then you can give me some responsibility". Lohia was making the Government cautious about the misdeeds committed by it. However, his objective behind this criticism was public welfare and not to gain power.

The closeness between Lohia and Gandhiji was increasing day by day. He loved Lohia, he was much impressed by Lohia's views of building better society, and at the same time, he wished to make the image of Lohia as an ideal for the country. One evening Gandhiji and Lohia were walking together. On the way Gandhiji said, "You smoke cigarettes and take many cups of coffee and tea in a day. Taking of tea or coffee in excess quantity causes many health problems. Smoking of cigarette is very dangerous for health". Gandhiji further said, "You should be a true representative of the people. By smoking cigarettes you cannot mix up with the people and become a true representative of them in a country like India".

Lohia was listening to Gandhiji's words very patiently. He was silent and did not utter even a single word. Gandhiji looked at him and said, "Do you want to say something"? But Lohia was quiet. Looking at him Gandhiji again said, "Do you want me to stop speaking any more"? Ultimately Lohia said, "No, it is not so, you may continue".

However, Lohia spoke very little on that day, though Lohia and Gandhiji, discussed other problems. After a few days, Gandhiji came to know that Lohia had left the habit of smoking cigarettes. After hearing this news Gandhiji became very happy and his love and respect for Lohia further increased.

Murder of Gandhiji

In the last week of January 1948, Lohia passed most of the the time with Gandhiji. During that period, they discussed various problems of the people of different states. Meanwhile, a strike of the labourers was going on in Bombay. Hence, as a result of that strike there was a great disturbance amongst the labourers which was instrumental in causing huge loss in the production of the country. Lohia collected detailed information about that strike. He worked out the reason for that strike and thought about the expected solution. Lohia met Gandhiji on 25th of January and he wanted to have a discussion with Gandhiji about the strike. But Gandhiji told Lohia that he would discuss that matter with him, in detail, after one or two days. On January 28, Lohia met Gandhiji again. Gandhiji asked him to come to his bedroom as he wanted to discuss various matters with him. Gandhiji was still busy. After some time Lohia went to him and told him that he wanted to sleep for a while. However, he requested Gandhiji to awake him after some time. In the morning when Lohia got up as usual Gandhiji had left for the morning walk. Lohia felt much sad about it. After coming back from morning walk

Gandhiji said to Lohia that as he was sleeping soundly he did not think it proper to awake him. Gandhiji further said that, "Tomorrow I would discuss this matter with you in detail as he wants to determine something between Congress and the socialist party". As such, he instructed Lohia to come on the next day and they would "talk a lot".

On January 30, at the appointed time in the evening, Lohia took tea and left for "Birla House" to see Gandhiji. On the way, he got the tragic news about the murder of Gandhiji. On hearing that sorrowful news, Lohia became dumbfounded and stunned. He could not understand what to do now. The words of Gandhiji "We would talk a lot" were haunting his ears. When he reached Birla House, thousands of people were present there. The dead body of Gandhiji was lying in a room. Lohia thought that he had become an orphan because, after the death of his father, he got the love and affection of a father from Gandhiji. Gandhiji used to say, "Now Hira Lal is no more but he is alive". It was an irony of fate that Gandhiji had been a preacher and messiah of "non-violence" throughout his life, ultimately had to become a target of "violence". Lohia was very perplexed and his heart began to sink. He had never thought of India without Gandhi. Lohia was proud of the Indian culture. When the dead body of Gandhiji was placed in a Military truck, a large number of admirers mounted on the truck wearing their shoes but Lohia asked them to put off their shoes.

It was decided that the ashes of Gandhiji would be immersed in Holy Ganges in Paryag after twelve days. The ashes were to be carried there by a special train. A large number of people from every walk of life such as farmers, labourers, traders, students, including old men, women and children were standing on all the stations, en route to Paryag, to pay their last homage to Gandhiji. The scene at these railway stations was very pathetic. Most of them were so emotional that tears were running from their eyes. They showered flowers on the train.

Lohia had formed the Nepal Congress on the advice of Gandhiji. That party was struggling against the monarchy in Nepal. The former President of Nepal Congress Mr. Vishveshar Parshad sat on the "fast till death" on May 25, 1949 as a token of their agitation. A meeting of the socialist party was held in Cannaught Circus where its members presented their views for helping the Nepal Congress and they passed a resolution unanimously for the immediate release of the Nepali leaders. Consequently, they proceeded to the Nepalese Embassy in the form of a procession for handing over that resolution. Dr. Ram Manohar Lohia who had become a prominent figure of India at that time led the procession. However, they were stopped 50 yards before the Nepalese Embassy and were not allowed to proceed further. Dr. Lohia asked the police that their procession was peaceful and they had come only to hand over a memorandum to the Ambassador. Nevertheless, police was strict on that point and asked them to disperse immediately. Consequently, they sat on the road and started raising slogans about the release of the Nepalese political leaders. After half an hour, the police resorted to lathi charge and shed teargas. As a result of this high-handedness of the police many people were injured. At night, Lohia was arrested and locked up in the Parliament Police Station.

On the next day, contrary to his expectations, he was sent to the jail. There were 50 persons with Lohia including two girls and two children. Lohia issued a statement, "The British Government had misbehaved with me many times but the shameful act of throwing tear gas was done by the Government of Independent India".

However, he was released on bail on the next day and June 2 was fixed up for hearing. That incident was published in the leading newspapers of the country and some political parties criticized the same. The socialist leaders opposed that incident and it was decided to observe June 4 as the Protest Day. The Government took that matter seriously. Their bails were rejected.

On June 7, when the Court started the proceedings of the case a big crowd had gathered outside the court. Therefore, it was decided that in future the hearing of the case will be done in the jail. The case lasted for two months and ultimately everybody involved in the case was awarded two months imprisonment along with fine of Rs. 100 each. During the period Lohia remained in jail, he gave directions to his party workers as well as to the Nepalese Congress. The people of Nepal were given different type of relief and it became possible only due to the struggle of the Nepalese Congress. On June 20, "Lohia Day" was celebrated in all the big cities of the country like Calcutta, Delhi, Allahabad, Madras, Patna, etc. Various meetings were held on this day and the speakers strongly criticized the Government.

As Lohia's bravery and his work had been a matter of

discussion throughout the country to the extent that a number for programmes were chalked out to honour him. However, Lohia did not give much importance to such programmes and he did not agree to go for such programmes. He wanted to do many important works and he had very little time for the same. During that period, Hira Lal Lohia Library was opened in Kanshipur and a "Seva Gram" was established in Dacca as a token of services rendered by him for the welfare of the society, while remembering Ram Manohar Lohia, an hospital, a school and a rest house were housed in this Seva Gram.

Meanwhile, most of the countries of the world had been divided in two groups; one group was pro-America and the other group was Pro-Soviet Union.

The Socialist Party of India was minutely studying the foreign policy of both the groups and it was of the opinion that the newly independent countries should not support any group. Rather they should form a third, i.e., non-aligned group. The main objective of the newly independent countries should be to develop economically and become equal to the developed countries. Lohia viewed that India should not raise the Kashmir at U.N.O. The newspapers of Soviet Union criticized Lohia and called him pro-American. As Americans were trying to enter into Korea, but Lohia opposed it and explained that the membership of this third group should not be limited only to Asian countries rather European countries like Yogoslavia and Sweden should also be made its members. He further made it clear that the main objective of the third group should only be the welfare of the people of those countries.

Though the people belonging to Socialist Party were small in number, but they were scattered in all parts of India. Lohia wanted to strengthen the Socialist Party. In March 1949, he called a session of the Socialist Party in Patna where he put a proposal for strengthening it and gave the slogan of "go ahead" to the party. During that time Lohia was very much worried about the economic conditions of the country. He thought that there was shortage of capital in India whereas the number of the workers was very large. He felt that there was an urgent need to increase the industrialization in the country and the small machines should be used in those units so that more employment opportunities might be created. In that conference Hind Kissan Panchayat was formed. Though the political change had taken place but there was a need to do a lot more on the economic front for which the Socialist Party was continuously making the efforts.

In July 1949, Lohia was invited at Stockholm in connection with the issue of World Government. He was India's representative in that Conference but at that time, he was in jail. After his release from the jail he went to Stockholm. The Conference about World Government started on September 1. At that time, Lohia presented his views for remaining away from the two groups of the world, i.e. Capitalist and the Communist. He considered that the solution of international problems lied in the World Government and he had sympathies for the non-aligned. After the conference was over, he went to many other cities. However, he was more interested to visit Berlin City where he had been a student for four years. He had a number of friends in Berlin and from that city he got the international consciousness. Therefore, he reached Berlin *via* Copenhagen, Hamburg, Hanover and Bonn. He saw that after sixteen years Berlin had changed a lot. The old buildings had vanished. New buildings had been constructed at the places of restaurants and hotels where he used to take meals and tea. He enquired about his old classmates but he could not find them as many of them had left that place.

However, he got the address of one of his classmates, viz., Verner Attorn. At that time he was living at Frankfurt. So he went to see him and after reaching his house he came to know that many of his classmates had expired. He began to remember his friends; their talks, their hobbies, nature and he remained sad for a long time. After that, he visited other cities of England, West Africa, France and certain West Asian countries. In those countries, he addressed different meetings of journalists, students, teachers, trade unions. He also explained his views through radio talks. He made a good impression of himself through these lectures.

Efforts for Economic Freedom and Jail

On November 25, 1949, a big rally was arranged in Lucknow as a protest of the issue of enhancing the land revenue ten times than earlier in U.P. About one lakh farmers attended this rally. People were standing on both sides of the river Gomti. After some time they proceeded towards Legislative Assembly in a procession. Ram Manohar Lohia led the procession. Acharya Narender Dev was also along with him. They pasted the charter of demands on the gate of the Legislative Assembly. On the next day, news items appeared in the newspapers to the effect that a party has emerged against the Congress and discussions regarding that rally were held for many days.

Consequently, the meetings of the different bodies of the party were held in different parts of the country. At certain places the memorandum about the local problems were presented to the representatives of the people. Regarding the problems of the farmers, a meeting of the farmers was held on the request of "Hind Kissan Panchayat" and it was also decided to hold the National Conference on February 26, 1950 in Rewa. After the rally of Lucknow, the Government had become very cautious. The

Government did not want that such type of rally, which was a grand success, may be organized again. Therefore, the Government tried to create obstacles in its arrangements. The number of buses going towards Rewa was reduced and the pipelines supplying water to the city were cut off. However, in spite of these hurdles, the farmers participated in that rally in a large number from far-flung places. Lohia was much annoyed. He criticized the Government for its meanness and at the same time congratulated the people who had come on foot and did not care for water. Different views were expressed for making the prosperity of farmers in 5 lakh villages of India. Lohia said, "The people who live in our villages are not the poor farmers, rather they are the founders of the culture". Different views were expressed for uprooting the poverty. All these programmes had been the subject matter of news items in the papers for so many days.

In the beginning of 1957, Ram Manohar held meetings in the different states of India for chalking out constructive programmes of the Socialist Party and later on, it was decided to stage a demonstration as "Jan Divas" in Delhi under the chairmanship of Dr. Ram Manohar Lohia. So he became busy for the success of this programme. He consulted his party men living in different cities of India. Lohia propagated that there was a huge shortage of capital in the country and the hard working people could meet that shortage. He made up his mind to start certain community based projects from April 20 to May 17. The plan was to be chalked out by Lohiaji and he was also required to inspire the people for the said project. Lohia said to people "Today the sun of the constructive work of the party will arise. There is no need of capital at the initial stage as only the voluntary and community labour will be required". Under this project, different works were to be done to increase the infrastructure for the public welfare in different areas. Those projects were inaugurated by Dr. Lohia in Bulandshahr where the people were required to dig up a water channel for irrigating 300 acres of land. Similarly, the other social projects were also initiated.

"Jan Divas" was celebrated on June 3, 1957 in which lakhs of people from all over India took part. Those people went to Raj Ghat and undertook fast and vowed to undertake fast in future also on that day. The people of Delhi were surprised to see such a large gathering. The people raised slogans in the procession as "Give employment, food and clothing or leave the rule (*Rozi, Roti, Kapda Do Nahin to Gaddi Chhor Do*)". Ultimately, Lohiaji presented a charter of six demands to the President of India.

Meanwhile, wherever any problem of the farmers or labourers arose, Lohia reached there immediately and found out a proper solution for that. In those days, an incident happened in Kagdu village of Mysore. A landlord was the owner of 200 acres of land. However, 70 farmers were cultivating that land as tenants. He was paying land revenue to the Government at the rate of Rs. 2 per acre of land. He suddenly raised that revenue to Rs. 30 per acre. Ultimately, the farmers were unable to pay that huge amount of revenue. So he ousted those farmers from his land. The Socialist Party of Mysore helped the ousted farmers and consequently a movement was launched, as a result of which about 400 farmers were arrested and sent to jail. Lohia was going to join that movement. However, he was arrested at the Sagar Railway Station and was sent to Bangalore. Lohia made a *habeas corpus* writ against his arrest. The farmers became very annoyed and they held many conferences in support of Lohia.

It was decided to observe July 1st as "Protest Day" against the arrest of Lohia. Various meetings and rallies were arranged on that day. By that time, Lohia had become a very popular figure at the international level also. On that day people also demonstrated in front of the Embassy of India in London. Lohia received many invitations from different countries but because of that incident he had to change his programmes. Ultimately, he was released and after his release from jail he made a programme to visit America. Before his departure he held a press conference at Patna in which various questions about India as well as about International politics were asked from Dr. Lohia. The Press reporters were so impressed by his answers that those were published in many newspapers. In one of the papers it was written, ".......Lohia is simpler than an Indian farmer and sharper than an American youth. After looking at his uncombed and ruffled hair, bearing of his torture in the Lahore Fort and his determination and faith on non-violence proved true... after Gandhi, Lohia is the true Gandhian."

In July 1951, a All World Conference of the socialists was held at Frankfurt. Lohia represented India in that conference. In his speech Lohia said, "Two-third of the world is living on the brink of horrible poverty...... The rich countries want to usurp their wealth... We have to uproot the feudal and capitalist system of the society. There is also a caste system in the international sphere, where there are five big nations. Peace will be possible only if there is equality among all the nations".

The socialists, all over the world, became very much impressed with the views of Lohia as well as with the contribution he had made for the welfare of the society. So he became a popular figure amongst the socialists all over the world. After attending the conference at Frankfurt he visited some other countries like America, Japan, Thailand, Hongkong, Sri Lanka and Malaysia and expressed his views in these countries which were published in the newspapers of those countries as well as in the international press.

Later on Lohia was called at New York where he was to address the students and to meet the American traders. In New York, he impressed upon the people and explained that, economic prosperity was very essential and a lot of work had to be done in the backward countries. On being asked at the airport, as to why he had come to America, he said, "I have been very much interested in the works of Lincoln and Jafferson since my childhood. I am attracted towards the people of America....I am not intelligent than anyone of you but I have come from an ancient country which is also a very strong country". He was invited in the Pisc University at the place of Nashvilley in Nanaccy Province. In addition to the students and the teachers, other intelligent persons were also present in the hall. Many people had come there to listen his speech considering him a philosopher of progressive thoughts. He said, "Had

Negroes been co-rulers of the political power for the last 400 years and Africa would have been free, the measures about philosophy and about this aspect would have been different". His speech was much appreciated. After his speech the hall continued to resound with the sound of clapping for very long time. In the same year, he was given an opportunity to speak from San Francisco Radio and his speech was listened by approximately 50 lakh people. In his speech, he laid stress on the point that food and freedom cannot be separated.

Being impressed by his increasing popularity through newspapers, Mrs. Pearl S. Buck, the great writer of that time invited him. As large number of students, Arab socialists and leaders of the Trade Union of America reached at the airport to welcome him. The Indians settled in America, the people of socialistic concept and the officials of the Indian Embassy were also present there. Mrs. Pearl S. Buck became highly impressed by his knowledge about literature. She was surprised that a man who had passed maximum time of his life in jail and who had been concerned with a number of movements regarding social and economic issues had a deep knowledge about literature. He had the honour to meet the wife of the former President of America Mr. Roosevelt and the famous scientist Einstein. Dr. Lohia wrote about the social, economic and cultural conditions of every country wherever he visited.

Lohia had gone in some other cities of America. Once he was speaking in a meeting and a tall youth came to him and said, "Alas! The leaders of America could speak like you". While he came back to India after visiting Mexico, after travelling various countries of the world, an idea came to his mind that the socialists of the world should come together at one platform and there should also be an organization of the socialists of Asian countries. For that purpose, he arranged a conference, viz., "Asian Socialists Conference" in Rangoon in collaboration with Burmese socialists. In that conference, socialists of India, Burma, Japan and Indonesia also took part. Lohia gave a very impressive lecture for the direction of uprooting poverty, hunger and sickness from the Asian countries.

Socialist Struggle

The First General Elections in India were held in 1952. Lohia did not want his party to contest those elections rather he was in favour of continuing the movement to establish the socialistic pattern of society. However, many leaders of his party were interested in contesting the elections. Some senior leaders of the party like Achhuta Patwardhan, Kama Dev, Aruna Asif Ali, Chatopadhyay, etc., had left the party before the elections. His very close associate Yusaf Mehrab Ali had expired. Socialist Party also contested the elections but faced a big defeat. Lohia did not bother about the defeat. However, he made a programme to reorganize and strengthen his party. He called the socialists from various cities of the country and organized their meetings. It was found out that many socialists, who had their past connection with Congress, had rejoined Congress. During this year, The annual Conference of the Party was held in Gujarat in which Lohia presented a new point of view and later on, his views were published in a form of a book *Wheel of the History*. In this book, he had expressed his views, "that every culture after reaching its zenith automatically becomes slow. This process is applied to the culture of every country. In that situation every developed society becomes resilient". Dr. Lohia's these views were discussed in the leading newspapers.

In 1952, the famous Gandhian of that period, Acharya Kirplani, T. Parkashan and Parfulla Chand Ghosh left the Congress party and they floated "Kissan Mazdoor Party". That party also contested elections but faced a big defeat. During that period, Jaya Prakash Narayan undertook a fast of 20 days and decided to shun the politics after breaking the fast. Therefore, Lohia had to come forward to continue the party affairs. Lohia had never wanted any office in the party. However, he had to lead the party for the sake of strengthening it. Afterwards, the workers of both Kissan Mazdoor Party and the Socialist Party had suggested for the merger of these parties because of their same programme and policies. Therefore, for this purpose, a common meeting of both the parties was held on September 24 and 25. In that meeting, in addition to the merger of both the parties, one common programme with common objectives was adopted. After the proposed merger of both the parties, a new party was established in the name of "Praja Socialist Party." While addressing the newly formed party, Lohia said, "As there is a need for establishing a Socialist Party, so there is also a need in the same proportion for the development of the self-power. There is a need of immediate struggle".

By that time though five years had passed since India's independence, however, it did not progress much on the economic front. Hence, Lohia began to openly criticize the

Government. Pt. Jawahar Lal Nehru was well aware of the popularity of Lohia. Hence, Pt. Nehru tried to attract some of the leaders of his party by offering them higher offices in Congress Party. He offered the offices of advisors to Acharya Narendra Dev, Acharya Kriplani and Jaya Prakash Narayan.

Ram Manohar Lohia had difference of opinion with Jaya Prakash Narayan and Ashok Mehta for a long time. The Party convention was held in Betul where they arrived at a compromise with these two leaders and ultimately Dr. Lohia accepted the post of Secretary in the party. But this compromise was not based on the policies, it was just the need of the hour for bringing about peace in the party. The situation was very odd because what Lohia wanted was not acceptable to Jaya Prakash Narayan and Ashok Mehta. Therefore, an uneasiness was creeping within the party.

Some wrong entries had been made in the land records of Azamgarh, against which movement of the farmers was going on. As a result of that agitation hundreds of farmers were in jail. Socialist Party was helping those farmers. On account of that agitation, the Secretary of the District Ghazipur, who belonged to Socialist Party, was belaboured inhumanly to the extent that he was struggling for his life at a hospital of Varanasi. Lohia went to enquire about his health in the hospital. There he was honoured with the title, "Brave of Ghazipur". He raised his voice against the police atrocities in a huge rally arranged at Azamgarh and also criticized the high-handedness of the police at various places. During that time, a police officer slapped a Member of Parliament of this party and students were also fired in Lucknow. Lohia went to both the places and criticized the police and the Government.

The first convention of Praja Socialist Party was held on December 29 to 31. All the senior socialist leaders, like Dr. Lohia, Acharya Narender Dev, Acharya Kriplani, Ashok Mehta, Jaya Prakash Narayan, etc. participated in that convention. Dr. Lohia was elected General Secretary of the party against his will. Lohia presented a resolution for the purpose of establishing a socialist society in the country. Later on that resolution became so popular that it came to be known as Lohia Thesis. In this resolution, he explained in detail about the four pillar Government, decentralization, economic equality, agricultural and industrial policies, human rights as well as women rights.

In 1954, the rates of the canal water were raised in U.P., that matter was reported to the executive of the party. The party started a non-co-operation movement in 13 districts where the rates were raised. Dr. Lohia led the movement. About 1500 farmers, were arrested who had taken part in that movement. In those days, Lohia visited various places with the objective to create social awareness among farmers and labourers. On 4th of July 1956, Lohia made speeches at Kishanganj and Farookhabad and on the same night he was arrested while he was taking his meals. Thereafter, he was sent to Farookhabad jail. Lohia appealed in High Court against his arrest. En route to Naini Jail, he stopped for some time at Allahabad railway station where he met so many party workers and press reporters and openly criticized the Indian Government. Two judges of the High

Court, viz., Justice Misher Lal Chaturvedi and Justice S.C. Desai heard his appeal. Thousands of persons gathered in the High Court to see Lohia. A famous advocate Shri Satish Chander defended Lohia and Mr. Ghanyia Lal was the prosecutor in his case. However, Lohia presented his own case in the court. He said, "Here I am not a sinner rather I am appearing as an applicant". He further said, "It is the first time that I have been arrested for making a speech. The Special Power Act of 1932 under which I have been arrested is against the constitution of India. It is a sword of the imperialism and I hate the jail." On that day, it was hoped that Lohia would be released but there was difference of opinion between the Judges. Therefore, the case was transferred to a third judge, viz., Justice Chander Bhan Aggarwal.

The next hearing was fixed for August 24, 1954. On that day, again the people in thousands came to see Lohia and to hear the proceedings of the court. In his defence, Lohia quoted the examples of Socrates from Greece, Henry David Thoro from America and Mahatma Gandhi from India. He said, "these great souls had broken the laws of the society for the larger interests of the humanity and all these three philosophers had persuaded a large number of people to break the law". He further said, "I have not broken any law rather I have raised the voice against the Special Law".

On this, Justice Aggarwal announced the historical verdict and said that Article 3 of the Special Power Act of 1932 is against the Constitution of India 1950. He said, "I fully agree that the basic condition of a successful democracy is to ensure that its citizens are following the laws. In my opinion our Constitution protects the rights of every Indian citizen in connection with propagation of civil disobedience." As pursuance of that law, Dr. Lohia was released on August 28 alongwith 1000 other agitators. He was much annoyed over this imprisonment. He felt very tired. Coming out of the jail, he thought for going either to a hill, a sea-shore with his friends, as he wanted to rest for some days.

When Lohia was in jail, he received news about a police firing on a crowd in Kerala where seven persons were killed and many others were injured. During that period there was the Government of the Praja Socialist Party in Kerala. Lohia became very sad over that incident and he sent a telegram to the C.M. Mr. Pattam Thanu Pillay that reads, "The hooligans may be on the wrong side, and they too would have created a critical situation. Nevertheless the killing of people, in police firing, is absolutely a barbarous and mean act. A Non Government Enquiry Committee should be appointed and at the same time the Government must resign". A copy of this letter was sent to Shri Acharya Kriplani, the President of the Party. Though he was behind the bars, still he thought that his letter shall create commotion and the party would take it very seriously. He also thought that when the Chief Minister was taking that responsibility than who should resign? However, when he did not receive any reply until August 17, Dr. Lohia wrote a letter to the President of the Party to that effect that, "Being in jail and remaining absent from the meetings of the party, I thought to resign from the Office of the General Secretary of the party but now I want to resign from the executive also. I have received no reply from the Chief Minister. Kindly accept my resignation and get it published also".

Lohia had written this letter with great annoyance. He had a great sympathy for those innocent persons who were killed in the firing. He considered it a tyranny and brutality on the part of the Government to have fired on those unarmed and innocent people. Till August 23, he did not get any reply. He again wrote a letter to the Party President. However, he did not receive any reply again.

After coming out of the jail, he received two letters from the party President. In the first letter there was no answer of his letter but in the second one his views were appreciated and he was asked to present his views in the executive of the party. Though Lohia had resigned from the Executive of the party yet many other people, suggested him to present his views in the Executive. In response to that letter he said, "Either I am not fit for any office of the party or the party is not of that cadre to which I may become its Secretary".

The meeting of the executive of the party was called on September 4 and 5 at Delhi. Though Lohia's resignation was not accepted, however, he did not want to attend the meeting. Nevertheless, so many of his associates wanted him to attend that meeting so that he might be able to give his views and persuade the party workers to do some constructive work for the welfare of the society. However, Lohia was determined to speak against the party as well as the Government. He said, "As life for life logic is considered while giving verdict in a murder case, the same logic should be applied against the police officials who committed a heinous act of killing innocent people".

In that meeting Lohia's statement on the issue of Kerala Government was very much criticized by the party leaders. These were the views that Lohia had levelled false allegations on the Government. When senior leaders such as Sucheta Kriplani, Ashok Mehta and others were criticizing him, Jaya Prakash Narayan came out of the meeting though he was speaking in his favour.

Because of difference of opinion, the convention of the party was fixed on 26th to 28th September. The issue of firing arose again. Ashok Mehta, a prominent leader, spoke against the resignation of the Kerala Government. Some of the leaders were in favour of the Judicial Enquiry. Lohia said Judicial enquiry is a separate issue whereas the resignation of the Government is a separate matter. Mr. Pattam Thanu Pillay, Chief Minister of Kerala also presented his case. Ultimately, the voting held on that issue. In that voting, 217 votes were polled in favour of the resolution and 303 were polled against it. As a result of that he resigned as a member of the Executive. There was a need to make certain changes to strengthen the party. A large number of members of the party were of the view that Acharya Narendra Dev should be elected as President. But he said that he would accept the Presidentship on the condition that Dr. Lohia would continue to be in the executive. In 1955, Congress secured the majority in the State Legislature defeating the Socialist Party and formed its own Government. Hence, the only non-Congress Government in India was ousted from power.

Meanwhile, Congress propogated for the establishment of the socialist society and it passed a resolution to that effect in 1955. Consequently, some of the socialists came closer to the Congress. Mr. Ashok Mehta said that they should welcome the resolution of the Congress. Lohia said in a statement that the party should welcome the resolution that Congress has come closer to the socialists.

Meanwhile, the Congress leaders tried to cash the statement of Mr. Ashok Mehta. As such, Congress leaders started propagating that they were also promoting and adopting the socialism. Lohia very well knew that by merely making a resolution without changing the social structure the socialism could not be established. Therefore, Lohia made a statement, "The people who believe in socialism as propagated by the Congress could join that party." In the meantime, Madhu Limay severely criticised Ashok Mehta. However, as a result of that criticism, he was suspended from the party membership in its Conference held at Bombay. Subsequently, he appealed to the National Executive against his suspension but his appeal was rejected. Lohia felt aggrieved over it and he supported Madhu Limay.

The socialists invited Madhu Limay in various cities of the country. He was honoured everywhere and he was also assured all kind of help. During that time, U.P. Unit of the party invited Limay in Ghajipur Convention and honoured him. Consequently, the national executive of the party dissolved the executive of Uttar Pradesh Unit and the proceedings of the U.P. unit were declared null and void. Afterwards that act of the National Executive was not considered proper in so many states and Lohia decided to launch a movement against the national executive of the party. The youth wing of the party scheduled its conference at Puri from 29 to 31 of May. The youth wing of the party invited Madhu Limay in the capacity of their President and along with him, they also invited other leaders like Acharya Narender Dev, Ashok Mehta and Dr. Lohia, etc. Nevertheless, the General Secretary of the party wrote a letter to the office bearers of the party directing them not to attend that conference and as a result of that letter no other leader except Lohia attended that conference.

In such a state of affairs, Lohia was deeply sad over the leadership of the party. There were a number of problems of the farmers and labourers in the different states of the country. Dr. Lohia was persuading the leaders of the party to take interest in such problems, but party leadership was not taking any interest in those problems. Meanwhile the party had started an agitation against the Government of Manipur and after reaching there, Lohia held a big rally without taking the permission from the Government. A large number of people came to hear his views. However, just before the conclusion of the rally, Lohia and six other leaders were arrested. Dr. Lohia was locked up in a very small cell. He was also insulted. Lohia made a *habeas corpus* writ and was released because of that writ. Nevertheless, as soon as he came out of the jail gate, he was again arrested. He again made a *habeas corpus* writ and was again released. That this time the Magistrate had fined Rs. 25.

After his release, Lohia started to think seriously about strengthening the party. As the party has become lazy, he was not satisfied with its functioning. Therefore, he started to form a new party. Dr. Lohia was interested in the economic progress of the country but he thought that little progress had been made in that direction. He concluded that the human rights were also being violated in different parts of the country. The Progressive Socialists welcomed the idea of floating a new party by Lohia. On December 31 and January 1 of 1956, the convention of the new party was organised at Sandhi Bela and a red flag of the party was hoisted. A conference of 1200 young socialists was also arranged in Hyderabad at the call of Dr. Lohia. Dr. Lohia gave a historical speech in this conference. He said, "There is no need that a socialist may be called a Gandhian or Marxist. On the path of non-violence, sometimes the side of non-violence becomes heavy and at other time, the side of revolution becomes heavy. We should leave neither non-violence nor revolution. The socialist movement should be made intensive until the ultimate war against exploitation is won". The leaders included in this party were Gopal Narain Saxena, Vijay Ram Raju, Mani Ram Bagri, Raj Narain Singh, Gopal Saxena, Baleshwar Dayal, Rabi Rai, etc.

In August 1956, Lohia launched a journal known as *Mankind* from Hyderabad with the objective to propagate the programme of the party. Lohia was its Chief Editor. Lohia managed to send this journal to the different units of the party in the different states. The research-oriented papers on economic, social and political affairs of the country were published in that journal. The new party organized a procession of about two miles long, i.e., from the Gomti Nagar to the Council Hall in Lucknow. The people of Lucknow were already familiar with the organizing ability and popularity of Dr. Lohia. Most of the papers in the country published the news items and comments about this procession. The second general elections of the Parliament were to be held in 1957. Lohia wrote letters to all the office bearers of the party to protect the Constitution of the country. Although, the party workers were very rigid yet their number was very small. Therefore, he wrote them to have cooperation of the party workers in the states having same point of view. Lohia put forward his views. He said, "Socialist Party wants to change the ideology. The party cannot bargain its high ideals for the sake of getting some seats". At the same time, Praja Socialist Party was also of the view that all the parties having same ideologies should come at the common platform.

The first convention of the Socialist Party was organized from December 28 to 30 at Sihora. A large number of people from all over the country attended that conference. Lohia felt that true and sincere people who wants to do their best for the party, did not speak much but, on the other hand, sycophants used to make tall speeches in the meetings. Therefore, he found a solution for that. He made his speech on 28th but on 29th he deliberately did not appear in the convention so that everybody might speak with open heart. However, he wanted to know the opinion of everybody. For this purpose he made a plan that he may know the views of everyone and accordingly he attended the evening session.

Afterwards, in his Presidential address he said, "There are three measures to change the society, i.e., law, propaganda and example. Can the improvement be brought about in the country by the cleverness? When the very foundation of the politics changes with the change in the minds of the people, under those circumstances only the changes can be brought about in the country".

Dr. Lohia had very little spare time in his life. However, whenever he found some time, he spent that time in reading and writing. He used to go through news items and articles in the newspapers. He felt that the views of Dr. Bhim Rao Ambedkar are similar to that of Socialist Party. Though he made sincere efforts to change the society but could not achieve desired success in that direction. He sent Mr. Goswami to Dr. Ambedkar for the purpose of merger of his faction into the Socialist Party. Lohia wanted that the views of Dr. Ambedkar might be propagated and practised throughout the country. This effort of Lohia might have succeeded but there was something else in the destiny and Dr. Bhim Rao Ambedkar expired.

The elections of 1957 were imminent. Dr. Lohia never wanted to contest those elections, but at the same time he eagerly wanted to strengthen the party. Keeping this fact in view, he wanted to help the candidates of his party so that they might win. However, the party workers were of the opinion that he must contest election of the Parliament. Therefore, he contested from the Chakia Chandoli Constituency of U.P. Lohia was the biggest opponent of the Congress. Hence, it employed all its machinery to defeat Dr. Lohia. Ultimately, he lost this election with the margin of 30-35 thousand votes. Losing the election had no significance for Lohia. He kept himself busy in his work and continued to criticize the extravagancy done by the Government. He started a countrywide movement for providing grant of concessions to labourers and for removal of the land revenue on the land below 6 acres of holdings. As a result of this movement of Socialist Party, about 3,000 people went to jail voluntarily.

Jaya Prakash Narayan wanted the merger of Praja Socialist Party and the Socialist Party. For that motive, he met Dr. Lohia at Lucknow on July 15. However, on the issue of ideology this meeting could not bear any fruit. Both of these leaders also had a meeting at Calcutta in August but still the unity could not be brought about in the parties. In the same year, the Socialist Party launched an agitation for the removal of the statues of the Britishers. Consequently, the party workers were arrested and sent to jail. Subsequently, by 15th August the Government removed these statues at their own but the party workers who had raised that demand were not released from jail. Dr. Lohia remarked, "As Raj Narain has been awarded 18 months jail term for removing the statue in the same way, Sampurnanand should be awarded 29 months in jail term for ordering to remove the statues". Therefore, Dr. Lohia decided to launch an agitation for the release of the prisoners.

The Government of U.P. was determined to harass Dr. Lohia on one pretext or another and wanted to put him behind bars. On November 2, Lohia was standing in the Office of the Sales Tax in Lucknow. A mail carrier came there to deliver the mail, Dr. Lohia stopped him and very humorously said, "You should not have come to this office as because of the functioning of this office the prices of food articles increase". Consequently, according to the pre-planned scheme, he was arrested on a petty charge of interfering with the Government work. In this regard, though, the postal worker had stated that Dr. Lohia did not obstruct him in his work and he had distributed the mail without any interference. The Socialist Party decided to celebrate "Lohia Day" on November 16, as a protest against the arrest of Dr. Lohia. That arrest was discussed and condemned throughout the country. Lohia made an appeal in the High Court. The Magistrate went to the jail for hearing that case but Lohia refused to appear before the Magistrate because he was not allowed to see his lawyer. Subsequently, Superintendent of the Jail himself went to Lohia at 4.00 p.m. and threatened him to the effect that if he would not appear before the Magistrate at his own then they would take him forcibly. Lohia replied him calmly that as he had appealed in the High Court, you could not use force. The Superintendent went away and Lohia thought that perhaps he had agreed with his arguments.

However, within a few minutes the Superintendent, accompanied by Jail Warden, 30-35 Numbardars and about 50 prisoners again came to Dr. Lohia and they started beating him with sticks, blows and with shoes. He was also hit at his secret organs. Ultimately he was tied on a chair and he was dragged to a distance of about one and a half furlong. In this way, he was brought before the Magistrate. It was midnight and Dr. Lohia refused to say anything before

Magistrate. Afterwards Mr. Goswami, advocate of Lohia presented his case before Justice Raghbir Singh. The hearing of the case continued for three days. Lohia defended his own case and ultimately the Judge exonerated him from all the charges. However, Justice Bhalla had different views, therefore, the case was handed over to the third Judge. He also endorsed the views of Justice Bhalla. Consequently, Dr. Lohia appealed in the Supreme Court on December 21. The case was heard on December 23 and Supreme Court issued orders for his release. After his release Dr. Lohia was feeling much insulted and at the same time he was suffering with a number of physical ailments like High Blood Pressure, Heart Trouble, etc. He never bothered that some of his associates had become Ministers in the state as well in the central government. Some of his associates were Chief Ministers and some others had occupied high offices. Even Jawahar Lal Nehru, Prime Minister of India, who had at one time had great love and affection for Dr. Lohia. All of them must have read about his plight in the newspapers but nobody had bothered and he had to face the police atrocities. He was very aggrieved to think that neither he had been able to change the society nor he could be able to change the minds of his fellow citizens. About his failure, he was mentally upset as he was determined with his views that politics is a means of social service.

Lohia was invited in the various cities of the country. He went everywhere, attended the meetings and persuaded the people to establish socialism. In November 1958, Lohia was invited in some cities of Assam. He addressed the meetings at Gauhati, Dibrugarh and Jorhat, etc., and desired to go to NEFA. However, he was not permitted to go there. Meanwhile, the office bearers of his party sent a telegram to the Governor of Assam for allowing him to visit NEFA. In response to that, the Governor replied that he likes to see him but Lohia replied that he would meet him on his return from NEFA. Ultimately, Lohia was not permitted to visit there and he had to come back. However, he made a speech to the effect that next year he would come again and would enter NEFA. Although the people did not take his words seriously, but exactly after one year on November 23, 1959 Lohia entered into NEFA and he was arrested but he was released sending him out of NEFA. He wrote "I have no palace, nor gardens.... And he found big pleasure to see my country in different forms......"

Lohia was a combination of a revolutionary, social reformer, political leader, writer, a critic and philosopher and everything. He dreamt that socialist system would be established in India where there would be equality of wealth and the human rights including rights of women would be secured. He wanted to contribute a lot towards his country. Being impressed by his views a large number of people had joined his party but later on they deserted him. Among them, so many persons left him for the sake of gaining high posts in the Government. Under these conditions he alone continued with his mission and analysed the policies of the party. Not only this, he used to look after the work of the party also.

Lohia laid the foundation of socialism in India. Afterwards he made it strong and also advanced it. He was hopeful that one day he would definitely achieve his goal for which he had been dreaming since his childhood. He launched various new programmes from time to time to keep the people awakened. In 1960 he launched a new movement having four main objectives, i.e., removal of English, fixation of prices of necessary commodities, removal of caste system and protection of Himalayas. Lakhs of people in India participated in this movement.

Dr. Lohia visited various cities to attend the meetings of the party. Whenever he came to know that some injustice was being done to any section of the society at any place, he immediately went there. He took part in every genuine agitation whether the socialist party or any other party launched it. Usually he used to stay in Government Circuit House. On April 17, 1960, he stayed at the circuit house of Kanpur. However, as he had not obtained the prior permission for his stay in the circuit house, therefore, he and his associate Shri Jagdish Raizada were fined Rs. 100 each for this negligence. In 1961, he went to Madras to address in a meeting regarding *Angrezi Hatao* (Remove English) where some people attacked him and he was injured.

In this year he got invitations from the Socialist Parties of some countries including Rome (Italy), Athens and Cairo (Egypt). During that period Lohia emphasized that socialism should be adopted in whole of the world. His speeches were published in the newspapers of those countries. The intelligentsia of those countries also appreciated his views. The press reporters asked him many questions for a long time but he impressed them with his prowess.

The third general elections of India were to be held in 1962. Dr. Lohia again did not want to contest the elections. Rather he was interested to go on campaign tour in support of his party candidates so that they might be elected as members of the State Legislative Assemblies or the Parliament. But it was decided by the party that he must contest the election against Pt. Jawahar Lal Nehru from Phoolpur. At that time, Pt. Jawahar Lal Nehru was the Prime Minister of India and he was having enormous powers. It was considered that it would be miracle to defeat such a powerful person in the elections. Dr. Lohia was not afraid of contesting the election against Pt. Jawahar Lal Nehru. However, he was aggrieved to think that he had to contest the election against a person who had once great love and affection for him. He did not disclose his sentiments to anyone. One day before filling the papers he wrote a letter to Pt. Jawahar Lal Nehru.

"Dear President",

You would be surprised to read this letter. When I left the office of the Congress Committee forever I paid regards to that building. Aruna was with me. That was our last meeting.

In these elections, your victory is certain. But if the certainty is turned into uncertainty and ultimately to your defeat then I would be extremely happy and it would also be beneficial for the country. Then you would get the opportunity to improve yourself and become a better person. In the end, I pray for your long life so that I may get the opportunity to reform you.

Yours
Ram Manohar Lohia

After writing this letter, Lohia visited various places to campaign in favour of his associates. During the campaign he gave speeches at about 12-13 places every day where he explained the political and economic conditions of the country in detail. After a few days he got a letter from Pt. Jawahar Lal Nehru that was as follows:

> Dear Ram Manohar
>
> Received your letter without date and address. I am sending the reply at the address of Socialist Party, Allahabad.
>
> "I am happy that a sober person like you is opposing me in the elections. I think in this election the discussion would be centred on the political programmes. Be cautious and ensure that the personal discussion should be curtailed. On my part I promise that I would not visit my constituency even for a single day."
>
> Yours,
>
> Jawahar Lal Nehru

Subsequently the senior Congress leaders visited that constituency repeatedly. Even Nehru himself visited there for three or four times. Maximum efforts were made for the victory of Nehru. The Socialist Party workers also propagated about their policies at the different places. However, they had shortage of sources. To contest election against Nehruji was just like striking a mountain. Dr. Lohia lost the election but he secured many votes. At 43 centres he was ahead of Nehru with the margin of hundreds of votes. The famous American paper *Times* reported, "After casting every 2 votes in favour of Nehru one vote was cast in favour of the leader of the Socialist Party. The election of Phoolpur has made it clear that Nehru was not invincible."

As usual, Dr. Lohia was not affected by the defeat in the election. He immediately started his routine work in the direction of achieving his goal. He called a meeting of the party in which he emphasized his party members for achieving their objectives, i.e., the establishment of socialistic pattern of society, promotion of human rights and the rights of women, etc. He also encouraged them to work hard for achieving these objectives. Meanwhile, China attacked India on October 20, 1962. It was a great shock for Lohia and his associates. He encouraged the people by visiting various places of the country. However, Lohia was not satisfied with India's foreign policy as much area was in the possession of China. A large number of soldiers were killed during that war. Dr. Lohia elaborately spoke against the Government on November 11.

Lohia in Parliament

Dr. Lohia had neither desired to gain power nor it was the aim of his life to attain high positions. However, his only objective was to serve the society sincerely and to make efforts for its prosperity even though he had to suffer a lot in his efforts. He wished that politics should be the means to serve the society. His associates wanted Dr. Lohia to become a Member of Parliament. They thought that in that way he could be able to contribute more for the social welfare and setting up Socialist Society in India. They also thought that if he became a Parliamentarian then he would be able to raise his voice throughout the country as well as the world. In 1963, a bye-election was to be held in Farookhabad constituency. Lohia was compelled to contest that election. In that election, other opposition parties also helped Dr. Lohia and he won with a margin of 68,000 votes. At that time, the defeat of Congress was a matter of great concern. When Lohia entered in the Parliament, all the Members of Parliament stood up from their seats and clapped for his welcome. The people of Delhi arranged a function in Ram Lila Ground in the honour of Dr. Lohia. Thousands of people reached Ram Lila Ground to welcome him.

During the Parliament session, Dr. Lohia cautioned the Government about the growing poverty in the country. In a speech Lohia said, "The daily income of 16 to 18 crore of people in India is only 3 or 4 annas and this indicates that they are living the life of poverty". However, Nehruji insisted that their income was 15 annas per day. This controversy was widely discussed in the national and international newspapers. This controversy was known as 3 annas *versus* 15 annas. However, the main benefit of this controversy was that the intelligentsia, the students, the policy makers, politicians, etc. became anxious to know more about the reasons for the poverty in the country. On March 13, Lohia celebrated the "Janwadi Divas" in Delhi where lakhs of people participated from all parts of the country.

In May 1963, Lohia went on a tour of the eastern countries and after that tour he went to America. Tugal Southern College at Jackson, which was the centre of the human rights, had invited him on May 26 to address the teachers and students on the issue of human rights. He used to wear *dhoti*, *kurta* and chappals he visited everywhere in the same dress. A human rights activist Mrs. Rath Saltipan accompanied him. A number of people gave him a warm welcome at the airport. However, when he went to a hotel for taking meals, he was not allowed to enter in the hotel because of the racial discrimination. Ultimately, he had to come back without taking his meals. Nevertheless, he challenged the manager and said that he would come again tomorrow. True to his words, he went there on the next day and tried to enter the hotel forcibly. He was arrested immediately. However the next day he was released when his identity was disclosed. At the same time, the Home Department of America apologized from the Indian Embassy. In response to that Lohia said, "There is no significance to seek apology from me. The American President should seek aoplogy from the black people all over the world who are being badly treated and deprived of human rights by the white skinned people".

On May 27, Lohia was informed in America that Pt. Jawahar Lal had expired. Although Lohia had been a great critic of Nehru but he was shocked to hear the news of his sudden death. He sent a condolence message, "I am very much aggrieved over the death of Prime Minister of India and a great leader of the Congress. He was a person who represented our people on account of his love and affection towards them".

Dr. Lohia, whether he was in India or abroad, he was continuously getting letters from the associations, organizations, political leaders, etc. Since he had become a Member of Parliament, the Members of Parliament used to listen his views very attentively. There had always been something new in his speeches, which were appreciated not only by his partymen but also by his opponents. It was very interesting that even his opponents were appreciating him. People appreciated him because of his seriousness and thorough knowledge of different problems of the masses. He had critical thinking, independent judgement and direct approach to the central point. He was getting thousands of appreciation letters from all corners of the country. It was said, "Lohia appeared in the Lok Sabha like a storm".

Dr. Lohia was also a good writer and whatever he wrote was based on his personal experience. He and his followers wished to make Hindi as the national language of the country. He inclined to launch a movement against the caste system. Similarly, he was against the idea of having any relationship with Congress as well as with the Communists parties.

In those days, an idea came to his mind that the people who believed in socialism were very determined, therefore, they should come at a common platform after shedding their differences. He was of the view that Praja Socialist Party and Socialist Party should be merged as a one party. Therefore, he united both of these parties and Mr. S.M. Joshi was made its President. The first convention of that newly formed party was called at Varanasi from January 29 to February 1. Dr. Lohia made his best efforts to bring all the socialists of the world at a common platform for launching a worldwide movement to establish socialism all over the world. For this purpose, he got an invitation from the German Socialist Party. He went there, where he gave a programme to propagate and persuaded the members to promote socialism. His speeches were published and appreciated by the newspapers of the European countries. After Germany he went to Soviet Union and then to Afghanistan. In Afghanistan, his main objective was to see his former associate Khan Abdul Ghaffar Khan who was a great freedom fighter.

When he met Khan Sahib, he kept him in embrace for a long time and there were tears in the eyes of Khan Abdul Ghaffar Khan. Just like Lohia, he had contributed a lot to the freedom struggle and major part of his life he had been in the jail. He was also against the division of the country. The country was divided, he stood with his principles. He thought that in spite of being independent, no improvement could be made in the economic conditions of the country. He was of the view that people of his country were not enjoying human rights. Even after the formation of Pakistan, he had to remain in the jails of Pakistan for 15 years. During those days, he was staying in Kabul for his treatment. Lohia remained in Afghanistan for 4 days. Meanwhile he addressed some of the meetings and narrated about the contribution of Khan Sahib in the freedom struggle of India.

He wrote "We met each other after a long span of 18 years and it was very tragic scene. At the time of our meeting the tears were running down from the eyes of both of us".

In the meantime, exchange of fire took place between the forces of India and Pakistan in Kutchh area. He was to speak on Kutchh issue on August 9, at Patna but on the same day, a violent incident took place there and Lohia was arrested under the Security Act. Therefore, he could not speak on Kutchh issue. He made an appeal in the High Court and he was released subsequently. However, he was very sad and troubled to think over that his patriotism was being doubted.

Afterwards Indo-Pak war broke out in September. Lohia went to every part of the country and encouraged the fellow citizens. He advised the people to treat the Muslims as their brothers. He said, "Treat Muslim as brothers and have affectionate relations with them. However, be hard as a rock towards Pakistan." Consequently, there was cease fire. Russia mediated and a treaty was made between India and Pakistan in January 1966. However, Lal Bahadur Shastri, the Prime Minister of India expired at Tashkent and Smt. Indira Gandhi became Prime Minister of India.

There was no change in the socio-economic conditions of the country even after change of the Prime Minister and the Council of Ministers. The socialists created the awareness among the people on one issue or the other. In that direction, Samyukt Socialist Party gave a call for the "Bandh" on July 11, 1966. Once again, Lohia was arrested at the Agra station and his case was persued in the High Court of Allahabad. He remained in jail for many days. During that period, he studied the family life of the prisoners and the causes that forced them to commit crimes. He concluded that poverty was the root cause for the larger number of crimes as most of the prisoners belonged to the poor families. He became more distressed to know that one prisoner Tota *alias* babaji who was to be hanged after a few days. He had been in jail for a very long time and he was repenting on the crime he had committed. He had filled a bond also that his 10 bigha land might be sold out and its price money might be deposited in the security fund. Therefore, Lohia wrote a letter to the President to stop his hanging. In spite of his best efforts, he could not stop that hanging. Emotionally and psychologically, he was very much disturbed over that incident. He thought about the domestic conditions of so many people like him and he felt that there was an urgent need of bringing about a change in the society. He realized that even after 19 years of independence they had not been able to change the social set-up of the country. He was much perturbed and aggrieved over these thoughts.

Meanwhile fourth general elections were imminent in 1967. The political firmament was in a flux. Lohia was of the view that Congress would not be able to gain majority in these elections. Lohia visited various cities of the country to address the rallies of the opposition parties. Lohia again contested from Farookhabad and won. Again, Congress Party formed Government at the Centre but in many states it suffered a humiliatory setback. In many states, either the other parties or the joint front formed their governments. The non-Congress parties formed their Governments in Bengal, Punjab, U.P., Madhya Pradesh, Haryana, Madras and Bihar. It was the first time that the non-Congress parties got a chance to show their ability and to contribute in their own way. Lohia was called in a number of cities, where he was honoured and his leadership was appreciated at the national and international level.

Afterwards Mrs. Svetlana, daughter of Mr. Stalin, a former Prime Minister of Soviet Union, and wife of an Indian freedom fighter Mr. Barjesh Singh sought permission to stay in India permanently. She met Lohia at Allahabad but the Government of India did not pay much heed to her request and consequently she went to Switzerland. A discussion was going on this issue on March 21, 1967 in the Parliament. On this issue, Lohia said that there are two mothers of a person, one natural and the other motherland. She had desired to adopt our motherland after being upset from her natural mother. However, this mother has also declaimed her.

Lohia's Death

After being a Member of Parliament, Lohia's work had increased manifold. Apart from it, he had to travel very long distances in different parts of the country for the achievement of his objectives, i.e., establishment of socialistic pattern of society, promotion of equality between rich and poor and the promotion of human rights. These were his goals for which he was dreaming since his childhood. On the one side, he was to travel more and on the other side, he was having less time to take rest. He went to Patna and persuaded his old friend Mr. Jaya Prakash Narayan that he might become active again in politics. The hope also arose but Lohia was not feeling well in those days. He was tired but continued his work. His heart has become weak. He felt high blood pressure so he had to be admitted to the Willingdon Hospital of Delhi for treatment. He was having problem of urination so his prostate glands were operated but this news was not told to his associates.

However, the next day the news about his operation appeared in the newspapers. A large number of people came to enquire about his health in the hospital and they were informed that it was a minor operation. However, he would be kept in the hospital for a few days. Suddenly on October 2, his condition became critical. He was having high temperature and his pulse rate became rapid. Afterwards his blood pressure rose and he went in coma. Meanwhile he became conscious for two-three times but his condition became critical again. On the next day, the news about his illness published in the leading newspapers of the country. At that time, Raj Narayan was in Kabul and he rushed to Delhi. Jaya Prakash Narayan and his wife came from Patna accompanied by some senior doctors. So many parliamentarians, leaders of political parties including Sh. Karpoori Thakur, the then Minister reached the hospital. Doctors examined him. He was under the treatment of Dr. Wig who was a famous doctor of that time. By the morning of 3rd October, the condition of Lohia improved to a large extent.

However, on the same day some other complications developed. Suddenly he started to hiccup and the doctors could not control the same in spite of the best efforts. Mr. George Fernandes and Mr. Madhu Limay brought Dr. Kohalwala and Dr. Dastoor in the hospital who were experts for such problems. After thorough examination, it was found out that poison was spreading in his body. Doctors prescribed some medicines. However, those medicines were not available in India. Subsequently those medicines were brought from England. After his treatment, he was feeling some relief and it seemed that he would recover. However, on October 5 his condition once again became very srious. More medicines were brought from abroad, and some specialists were also called simultaneously from Bhopal, Varanasi, Patna and Lucknow. Subsequently, there was some improvement in his condition by October 7 and it remained stable. However, urea had increased in his blood. Mr. Madhu Limay sought the opinion of Dr. Richang of England, who was an expert of such problems. He was of the view that during the operation some injury might have caused and that was not healing up.

The doctors attending on him also agreed with the view of Dr. Richang and against the wishes of the Delhi doctors; they opened his body stitches again and cleaned his wound. The puss had gathered in the body that was flushed out. An American doctor of Ludhiana made a hole near his neck for the sake of his recovery. However, still there was no improvement in his condition. Thousands of people were standing outside the hospital who had come to enquire about his health. They were praying for his early recovery. Mr. Morarji Desai, the then Deputy Prime Minister, also came to the hospital. On October 10 a famous doctor of Germany Dr. Ilqaiel who was a specialist of these problems arrived in the hospital. All the doctors concluded that there was a cancer in his prostate glands. Dr. David opined that if he recovered from that situation then operation for cancer could be performed. Dr. Lohia was still in coma. The efforts of the doctors were proving fruitless. However, when he became conscious he just smiled. When Mrs. Indira Gandhi came to see him he said to Mr. Raj Narain "Make her sit, serve her with snacks, water". He said, "The doctors and politicians both are alike in our country as both are unaware about the problems". Afterwards he lied on the bed again and became unconscious. Whenever he beçame conscious, he looked here and there smilingly.

While looking at the team of doctors, attending on him only, he said loudly, "So many doctors only for me! There are crores of people in India who have not seen the face of a doctor". Outside the hospital, people who had come from all over the country were much worried about his health and were praying for his recovery. However, his condition was not improving. People from every occupation such as farmers, traders, security guards, rickshaw pullers, labourers, etc., had gathered. Right from the President of India, to a prisoner released from the Tihar jail came to know about his health. A poor woman of Dr. Lohia's village prayed daily for his recovery and she undertook fast. One of his old friends, came to Delhi after disposing of his tea stall. Everybody was worried about him. He was given blood for many days. Whenever the demand of blood arose, a long queue of donors was formed immediately. The deep love and respect of the people towards him was visible at that time. Whenever Lohia became a bit conscious, he tried to speak in semi-consciousness state, "What would happen with lakhs of people... what would happen with farmers.... what would happen with India..."

Whenever he became a little conscious, the doctors were hopeful that henceforth there would be improvement in his condition but after sometime he again became unconscious. So many times, he started saying in unconsciousness, "The major jobs are yet to be performed but what can be done by a single person". On October 11, his condition was better and it seemed that he would go on improving. It was winter and night becomes cold in those days. On that day, October. 12, 1967 his condition again became critical all of a sudden. His blood pressure became very low. The doctors were worried but nothing could be done and his elements joined their origin at 1.15. A doctor came out of the room and said, "Dr. Lohia had gone". As these words were spoken, the people attending on him like Jaya Prakash Narayan, Karpoori Thakur, Balkrishan, etc. became dumb-founded. They were looking at each other without uttering a single word. With his departure, a preacher of socialism had departed as a result the socialism had become an orphan. There was no opponent of the Government. Dr. Ram Manohar Lohia who was to make the Parliament as conscious has left forever and said good bye to this world. His long associate flag of plough and a circle of red colour became sad. The Messiah for the bright future of the unemployed, the poor, labourers, farmers and students had been deprived of them.

Lohia's Thesis

Political Thinking and Corruption

Lohia was in favour of decentralization of Politcal power. According to him; the centre, province. the district, and the village should have their own role to play in the economic development of the country. The power should be divided amongst these units and every unit should be independent to exercise its powers. He put the four-pillar structure of decentralization of power that meant the administration should be divided into four units and there should be the government of each unit at every place. He was also of the view that the post of the district collector should be abolished and his powers should be divided into different parts. The elected representatives should look after the administration at every place and there should be no provision for nominations.

According to him, for the establishment of socialistic pattern of society, four-pillar administration is very essential. In his opinion whenever any industrial/ agricultural unit or any other institution is nationalized it should be managed by these four pillars, i.e., the centre, the province, the district and the village panchayat.

Dr. Lohia viewed the problem of corruption was very serious. He wanted that strict action should be taken against the offcials who were indulged in corruption. He was also equally against the bad behaviour of the Government officials. According to him, corruption and the bad behaviour are the same things. For the abolition of corruption, his approach was very scientific and practical. In his view, "corruption starts from the upper level and it should be nipped at that level in the same fashion as an ideal lady starts cleaning the stairs from the top". He wanted to study the causes of corruption and find ways to remove them. While speaking on the issue of corruption in the Parliament, he repeatedly said, "I appeal to the respected members to be very conscious at the time of debate over the issue of corruption at the central level". He used to say sarcastically, "The members should not be annoyed with him rather their debate should be centred on the critical circumstances through which the country is passing". He suggested that over the issue of corruption they should not be emotional rather they should find the ways to uproot this evil. He was of the strong opinion that every effort must be made to abolish this social evil.

While criticizing the law and order situation of the country he remarks, "There is no rule of law and administration is running at its own. Either the laws are not appropriate or they are not being executed properly. That is the reason that when Government decides to take some action against a culprit; he/she immediately takes the shelter of law". In his view favouritism or distortion of law, according to one's stakes, are also the forms of corruption.

While distorting the laws, one accepts money or not, that is a separate issue but it is a form of corruption. Dishonesty alone is not corruption rather having shallow knowledge of any matter is also a form of corruption. In parliament also, dishonesty alone is considered as corruption but if we do not know our conditions in India as well as in the world and if we do not identify corruption we would not be able to uproot it". He was not satisfied with the steps taken by the Government in this direction. Meanwhile, a decision was taken to establish a Central Vigilance Commission. However, according to him it was not the solution. In his view, "The commission would identify the areas of corruption and would abolish them. Therefore, it is a precaution and the commission would punish the culprits. However, it is not the solution because the root cause of the corruption will still remain unknown".

He wanted to establish such a society where the evil of corruption had no place. The Central Vigilance Commission would try only to cure this evil and not to save from it. Therefore, this evil would not be removed only by treatment. According to him, "The Central Vigilance Commission will fail in its efforts because if an influential person comes in its ambit he will escape easily from its grip and the ordinary person will easily be trapped. This will be the main cause of its failure."

According to Dr. Ram Manohar Lohia, "Influential persons are adopting so many methods which are beneficial in their business and profession". He mentioned some of the methods being used by these influential people and his views were based on reality. According to him, "In India so many people will be punished under proxy and the Vigilance Department would be unable to check it". In this connection, he narrated an incidence that "When some of the people gave court arrests against prohibition, then large scale smugglers of liquor sent their own workers for courting arrests so that police and the Home Minister might be pleased and their illegal business might continue". He cautioned that The Central Vigilance Commission would have to face such problems.

Lohia made the people conscious particularly about the fact that they had been enforced to believe that corruption had become a part of their lives and we should not bother about it. He said amusingly that some of the leaders were saying, "We have been ruling the country since a long time and have filled up our bellies. We had earned enough money so people should cast votes in their favour. If they would cast their votes in favour of poor people they would try to collect money by all means". In this way, he made the people cautious and asked them to refrain from corruption. He further cautioned them that there was a great need to identify the perimeter of corruption so that they might be nipped from its root. He was in favour to take very strong steps to abolish corruption and he did not believe in making only encouraging speeches. He drew the attention of the people towards the Home Minister's statement wherein he said, "The solution of this problem can be made by saints and social organizations because they can create divine atmosphere as well as divert the feelings of the people". However, Ram Manohar Lohia was of the view that morality should not be limited to the saints only.

He felt that the modern economic and social life had become so complex that leaving it on the saints is no solution of the problem. Once he agreed on a resolution that maximum limit of pay of a Government employee or a Minister should be fixed at Rs. 500. However, later on he admitted that at that time he did not realize the fact that while the maximum limit of income of the doctors, traders or landlords had not been fixed, so it would not be proper to fix the maximum limit of the officials or Ministers. Such types of limits should be equal for everyone and only then, the social equality could be established in the country. In the present society, infested with corruption and greed, this problem should be examined in its total reality. Ram Manohar Lohia felt that the lives of our leaders were not so transparent. According to him, "A Minister who speaks more against the caste system gives more benefits to people of his caste". Lohia was not happy over this type of dual behaviour of the leaders.

Dr.Lohia took a critical view of the economic inequality in the modern society. There was a stark reality in Lohia's view that, "People of India wants to enjoy the standard of living like the people of Europe and America but they forget that the people of America and Europe have been able to enjoy this standard of living after consistently working hard for 300 years for the development of agriculture and industry. On the contrary, we want to enjoy such type of standard of living without making any development either in the agricultural or industrial sector, which will ultimately pave way for corruption in our society. There is a big inequality in our society and the amibition to enjoy the high standard of living leads to corruption". Dr. Lohia wanted to fight inequality as it bred corruption. He always advised that the views of Mahatma Gandhi should be adopted wherein he has inspired the people to lead a simple life and to fulfil one's duty with dedication.

Views about Economy

Dr. Lohia took the problem of population very seriously and suggested that solid steps be taken to tackle this problem. However, because of large-scale unemployment, he advised that there should be maximum use of the labour of the country for increasing the production. He also suggested labour intensive techniques for the increase in production. According to him if more capital is installed, more employment opportunities could be created. In India, the population is vast while there is big shortage of capital. Therefore, more stress should be given to increase the production and employment opportunities. He was of the view that capital should be installed in small units. As far as possible, the power-oriented machines should be used and large-scale units should be installed only where the large-scale techniques are required.

Dr. Lohia had a dream to adopt a socialistic pattern of society with economic and social equality without any difference amongst the income of its citizens. The planning should be made at the earliest for the development of the country. As per present practice, tall promises as well as efforts to please only a few classes should not be made. In our society there should be no place for tyrants and sycophants. The small scale units would be encouraged.

There should be no difference in the profits of agricultural as well as industrial products. and trade would be promoted. There would be no uncertainty in the prices of agricultural and industrial products. Particularly in the agricultural sector it would be kept in mind that difference of low prices and high prices at the time of harvesting and off season is removed. In this way the exploitation would be finished. He was in favour of altering the very basis of the five year plannings. He was of the view that modernization in the consumer goods should be postponed. He was also in favour of small scale units and small machines for development of economy. The plannings should be made in the interest of the lower and middle classes. The main objectives of the planning should be the supply of healthy food, increase in the number of educated persons and the provision of clean water throughout the country. The socialist party should make policies of taxation and expenditure in such a way that the prices of the common goods remain within the reach of the common people.

In the planning, the arrangement of the goods should not only be made for present necessities but for the future needs also for the welfare of the whole humankind. Ram Manohar Lohia was of the view that revolutionary people or reformatory associations cannot achieve such type of objectives. For the solution of inequality of personal income, it is not possible without the control of the income from all sides.

There is a wide difference of standard of living between the people of India and in American and European countries. To remove this difference he suggested uplifting the people of backward classes. He was of the view that in this way the whole of the population might be promoted gradually to the modern standard of living. It should be made clear in the planning that how these backward classes could be uplifted.

According to him, socialist party rejects the idea of unnecessary and attractive modernization of large-scale units and useless cottage industries. Socialism implies complete reorganization of the whole economy and social life of the country. Wherever necessary it recommends the large-scale units and the use of power oriented small scale units according to requirements. It is not proper that some of the people enjoy the standard of living at par with the people of America and Europe while the common person leads the life of backward and lower level. There should be no use of such type of modernization. His party was also against the unnecessary pomp and show at the secretariat, airports and hotels. The socialists had the prime objective to raise the standard of living of the whole population. He did not want a great deal of inequality among the people. Actually, Dr. Lohia was to adopt the planning that might be useful for whole of the humankind. As per Lohia, socialist life means that there is equality of opportunities and possibilities for everyone to lead a good life. Lohia's socialistic concept was different from that of communism. He was neither in favour of capitalist nor in favour of communism. He wanted to uplift the humanity from the deep ditch in which it has been pushed by the capitalism. Dr. Lohia thoroughly studied the European socialism where the welfare of humanity and all-round development of society were the main objectives. He was of the view that socialism should be democratic and the society itself should be responsible for the welfare of humankind.

Keeping in view the burden of huge population, Lohia's thinking was absolutely right because the European countries, Canada, America and Australia due to low density of population, production can be made by capital oriented techniques and modern methods. Therefore, the people of South Asia and African countries cannot compete with the people of European countries. Therefore, the people of densely populated countries should never follow their methods of production. He was of the view that it would be proper if science is linked with the atmosphere. He expressed that such machines should be invented that might fulfil the needs of the village and cities. He was in favour of developing the idea of decentralization proposed by Gandhiji. He wished that with regard to planning and ownership of industry, the political control should only be for the welfare of the humanity. According to him barring the big landlords, others are in favour of the establishment of socialistic system. In his concept, the main reason to give more importance to the farmers is that the large number of people were dependent on agriculture.

According to Dr. Lohia, the European socialism and communism considered industrial labourers as the main source of power and they did not give much importance to the peasants. It may be due to the fact that most of the persons in those countries were engaged in industrial sector. In those countries, the industrial labourers are the axis of the revolution and in his opinion in an economy like India farmer is the main basis of revolution. However, he was aware that in the western countries industrial workers alone were not to be the axis of revolution. Similarly, in India farmers alone could not be the axis of revolution. He viewed that in India and some other parts of the world, the farmers have undoubtedly played a major role for the betterment of the economy of their countries. However, everybody has also performed his duty. That is why the views of the farmers, the workers, the artisans and other manual workers should be given equal importance in bringing about the economic revolution.

Nevertheless as per his opinion, the struggle for establishing this new political and economic system should be peaceful. Dr. Lohia knew that many a time, views of two persons might differ with each other. According to him the soul of Indian people had been suppressed since centuries, therefore, there was a need to elevate their psyche. He opined that the war against poverty should be fought continuously with serious thinking. There is a need to provide the special chances for the people who had been denied those privileges earlier. Hence, to practise his views the party was floated in 1955 in which he nominated 60 per cent of the office bearers on various committees from the Harijan and Backward Classes including minorities and women also. To make his views more solid and to practise this point of view, he applied this system for the election of the members right from the Parliament to local bodies.

For the development of the backward classes, he wanted to do anything and for this purpose, he was not afraid of taking the risk of life. It was because of the fact that the people of upper classes occupied the higher seats in politics. He knew the persons who would become his enemies and what type of difficulties had to be faced. He really wanted to bring about equality in the Indian society. For the last 5,000 years 80 per cent of the people in India had been considered as second class citizens. Even the Marxists were of the view that he believed in caste system and preferred a particular class. Dr. Lohia did not have such feelings rather his only motto was to bring equality among the members of the Indian society, irrespective of their class and creed.

Socialism

Dr. Ram Manohar Lohia founded his socialist party for establishing the socialistic pattern of society. He played a big role for the development of socialist concept in Indian society and dreamt to establish socialism in the political and economic life of India. Dr. Lohia was a ray of hope for the poor, modest and downtrodden people. On his part he continued his fight for the upliftment of these people and it was also the sole mission of his life. He struggled very hard for bringing about the economic and social development of the backward classes as well as the women. Had his views been adopted, the Indian society would have been a model in itself in respect of economic and social development. There would have been peace, comfort and mutual sympathy in the society and the rate of growth would have been faster. According to him, socialism could have made India a developed country. Dr. Lohia laid three conditions to achieve socialism, viz., vote, jail and development. He meant democracy, struggle and creative activity for vote, jail and development respectively. As these three conditions were necessary for the Indian people at that time, they are still necessary in the present age in the same proportion. Dr. Lohia presented his views about them at that time and that showed his deep study and far-sightedness. On account of his inborn qualities of leadership, he can be compared with any great leader of the world. In the process of establishing socialism in India, certain other organizations like Samajwadi Yuva Jan Sabha, Hind Kissan Panchayat, Hind Mazdoor Sabha, Hind Mazdoor Kisan Panchayat and Samajwadi Mahila Panchayat (Assembly of Socialist Women) were also formed. These organizations contributed a lot to the political and social way of thinking. Mr. Sharad Yadav, Kamal Nath, Rabi Rai, Satya Pal Malik, Brij Bhushan Tiwari and Ram Shankar Kaushik, etc., who with the passage of time rose as politicians at the national level, had been the members of the Samajwadi Yuva Jan Sabha (Assembly of Youth Socialists).

When Congress Socialist Section was formed in 1934, those people had been the students in Indian as well as foreign Universities. They were well aware of the principles of socialism and they wanted to establish socialism from the core of their heart. At that time some of their associates also joined them. However, large number of the people who claimed themselves to be socialists did not join the socialism whenever the movement for its achievement was launched.

The other promoter of socialism was Acharya Narender Dev. He had a deep knowledge of ancient history as well as Sanskrit. He had deep awareness about the future structure of society and he was fully alert about the approaching problems. He was influenced by Buddhism and Hindu Philosophy that is why he got himself engaged as a teacher in an educational institution instead of adopting legal practice. On the one side, he was influenced by Marxism and on the other, by Gandhism. But he got himself associated with Socialism. At that time Mr. Ram Manohar was preaching Socialism. Dr. Narender Dev and Ram Manohar Lohia started a joint movement for the establishment of socialistic pattern of society. Dr. Lohia was considered as a big force behind socialism. Dr. Lohia was born in a small village of U.P. but he had his education in Berlin University. At that time there was much influence of fascism and it was having no rival in Germany. On the other side in Soviet Union, Stalin was the force behind Communism. However, both were at loggerheads. Stalin never wanted fascism to spread in the world. Communism was also spreading and the common man was impressed by it. Dr. Lohia preached in favour of socialism, though he had to face a number of failures in his mission but he was not a pessimist. He used to tell his followers that it might take 100 years for establishing a socialistic pattern of society. Hence, he was teaching the lesson of patience to his followers. He was aware that the people who had socialist, bent of mind had spread in all the villages as well as in the cities all over India and there was a great need to organize them at one platform. The political observers and analysts are of the opinion that the propaganda of socialism had decreased after his death because the socialists are organized under the different names of the socialist party. They are more concerned with only one factor that of vote while they have neglected the other two conditions jail or struggle and the constructive work. That is why the role of socialists in the democratic institutions is negligible. Even the communist parties lay more stress on votes and ignored the other two means for the socialistic set-up.

After 1974 under the leadership of Jaya Prakash Narayan, the idea of complete revolution was given and this complete revolution was a form of all-round revolution as given by Dr. Lohia. This movement spread throughout the country. The cause for launching of this movement was the imposition of emergency in India in 1975, as a result of which all the opposition leaders were put in jail. These leaders floated Janta Party from the jail and all the leaders joined it, whether they were having the similar views or not. The Janta Party secured a big success in elections. Ultimately Janta Party formed its Government also. However, as leaders of various parties had different views, they felt suffocated in the Janta Party. At the same time they wanted this coalition Government to continue so that they might contribute for the betterment of the party as well as for the country. Ultimately, on account of the interference of some other parties, this Government could continue only for about two and a half years. The socialist movement again fell to the same level as it was earlier. Though socialist parties were given power at certain time intervals but being in small number, they could not establish the socialistic structure in the society.

The only goal of other parties was to attain power and it was limited up to votes only. However, they made tall promises of establishing socialism, eradication of poverty, etc., but they left the other two means that of the struggle and the constructive work. Such parties neither had the objective to establish socialistic pattern nor did they suggest the means to achieve it.

At present Socialism is as necessary as it was earlier. The prosperity and better quality of life is based on such type of society. Lohia was of the view that if socialists had achieved much by the constitutional means in Europe, it could be achieved elsewhere also. He was of the opinion that the souls of Indians had been suppressed for hundreds of years, their development was essential. The women folk in India had continuously been depressed because Indian society had been male dominated. Dr. Lohia viewed that the psyche of women was also required to be developed. For this purpose they should be provided special opportunities and privileges so that they may realize equality with men in their social status.

Dr. Lohia dreamt about socialism, where there is political, economic and social equality. There should be development of human values and public welfare. According to him one true, fruitful relation is to be maintained in realities of life and consciousness. In these days, there is a control over politics of the people of more than one religion in many countries of the world. There is control of the people of different religions over the economy also and those countries are progressing fast. It proved Dr. Lohia's view that wherever there is liberalism in religion there is peace and unity and the rate of economic development of those countries is fast. He said, "In the Indian history, I do not know any period, in which when there was fanatic Hinduism that would have brought unity or prosperity. Whenever there was unity or prosperity, at that time there had been more influence of liberalism in Hindu religion".

After independence, the people's attention had been drawn towards other religious issues and the people forgot the real issues and the social inequality remained as such. Such religious movements do not serve the interests of all the humanity but it serves the interests of a small sections of the society and the real issues of the public remains behind whereas the real issues are to fight against poverty and for national reconstruction.

Some of the people of political history have told about the beginning of socialism in the Vedic literature and some have told it as the instructions of Jesus that is a matter of sometime ago. The modern socialism was started in 1830. The philosophers and writers of Europe had also given their views on socialism that seems to be similar to the Christian morality. But he was Karl Marx who coordinated these views and explained them through a scientific principle. Initially in 1864, Karl Marx has explained his socialism as different from the old socialism. However, one thing is true that all these socialists believed in international cooperation and equality of income.

The socialism was propagated well up to First World

War. Nevertheless, in this war the socialists had to take arms against the aggressions and exploitation. They were to protect their motherland. The socialists are still struggling against the aggressors. There would be improvement in the living standards of the labourers and they will gain power. In the Second World War Hitler and other fascist forces on the one side, and the England and its friends on the other side, tried to influence by their own ideas and this clash of ideas turned into war. The crores of people were killed. They became disabled; the shelters of sisters, brothers, mothers, fathers and children were killed. Fascism was defeated, democracy and socialism got victory and socialist view became more stronger.

Dr. Ram Manohar Lohia's concept of socialism was very clear and wide. In Indian politics, everybody talks about his progressive thinking and social equality, though the practice of his party may be far and far away from the preachings. To understand Lohia's socialism it is very essential to understand Marx and Jawahar Lal Nehru's socialism and then to understand their difference with Lohia's socialism. Once you talk about socialism the picture of the central economy of Soviet Union or the mixed economy and beureaucratic structure of Jawahar Lal would appear in your mind. As Dr. Lohia's concept of socialism, could not be practised anywhere so it would be different and unfamiliar concept of socialism.

In these days, the different political parties are expressing the views of Dr. Lohia. Samajwadi Party, Janta Dal, Samta Party, etc., are dreaming to set up a socialist society as was in the mind of Lohia. These parties promise to set up, this type of society before and after the elections. There are Lohia's followers in all corners of India. They are struggling and sometimes it seems that it was not far off and there is no delay in establishing the socialistic pattern of society.

The leader of Lohia's stature had not been there after the death of Dr. Lohia. The image of socialism has declined. There were so many parties which were in favour to establish socialistic system but in this period, joining of this party or other had been going on and the role of such parties has become insignificant. These parties could not extend their concept and could not propagate. The concept could be extended by making the use of the principles of socialism and by applying them in social and political life. To propagate any ideology, some short term and at the other time the long term policies are required to be formed. But after the death of Dr. Lohia his followers could not achieve much success in their objectives as it was expected.

In these days when the socialism has broken down in Soviet Union and East Europe and other countries there is a feeling among some people that the idea of socialism has become useless. But here one point is to be made clear that there is a difference in socialism and communism. Lohia's principle of special privileges is a part of the principle of breaking of caste. The casteless and sectionless society were the particular principles of Lohia's concept of socialism and it was the special identification of his socialism. In East European countries, where the socialism has broken down, certain parties in those countries have changed their names as socialist parties. There are so many socialist parties in

Europe, those parties believe in democratic socialism. Those countries are Spain, Portugal and France where these parties had their governments. Whatever may be the form of socialism but it would have economic and social equality, social security, peace, democracy and prosperity and Dr. Ram Manohar Lohia had dreamt about such socialism.

It was only the Socialist Party that had broken repeatedly. The Communist Party got separated in two parts in 1964 and Communist Party (Marxist) became an important party and played an important role in the politics of India. Similarly, Jan Sangh and Congress had also played important role after their breaking down. Later on communist parties broke in other parts. They have their different names also but the basis of their principle had been the same that of Marx and Lenin. But it is very strange that Socialist Party even based on one principle and even with better leadership got scattered so many times, though it achieved some success. While analyzing the causes of its breakdown, the conclusion can be drawn that it was because of its dependence on other parties and lack of self-confidence.

The number of problems arises in independent India that of the separatist challenges, rise of fanatic powers, social tension, rising prices, economic crises, etc. But while analyzing its reasons it becomes clear that it was because of the selfish interest of the bureauracy, middle classes, industrial houses, traders and the petty interests of the political parties.

After 1962, Lohia changed his style of functioning. Instead of going alone, he made up alliances with the other parties and he achieved some success. In the elections of 1967, the opposition parties achieved much success in the Central and State Assemblies and in some of the states; the opposition parties formed their own government. At that time, it was the beginning of the construction of the new society and it seemed that now the politics of India would realize development and transparency in its dealings. At that time, the Socialist Party had made its identification and there was a big role of Dr. Lohia in this identification. However, somewhat else was acceptable to the destiny. Dr. Lohia expired and it was a big shock and the turning point for the socialist movement. According to Mr. Madhu Limay, "Death of Dr. Lohia was not only a loss of the socialist Party but also of the nation as a whole". There is no doubt that if Dr. Lohia would have survived for some more time, there would have been a different form in the history of India. Nobody knows that if he would have survived more time he may have seen his dream becoming true or he would have died as a sad and frustrated man. Mahatma Gandhi died before him and Jaya Prakash Narayan after him. However, Lohia's views would be appreciated and the revolutions launched by him would continue.

After the death of Dr. Lohia, his followers could not remain united and this party went on breaking. Mr. Madhu Limay, George Fernandes, Raj Narain, Siri Dhar Mahadev, Mr. Joshi and Karpoori Thakur were his followers. They were working as a team but it is very sad that after his death they could not go together and the socialist movement finished altogether.

Though Lohia and his companions were having their politics but that was beyond their personal interests, those were for social welfare. But history has not justified their role. In 1977, the different Groups like Jan Sangh, Bharti Kranti Dal, Congress (O), Congress for Democracy and Socialist Party contested the elections on the one symbol under the patronization of Mr. Jaya Prakash Narayan who was a socialist leader. All these groups formed a single party as Janta Party. They adopted the common election manifesto. This party achieved much success. But because of the internal differences in the leaders of the party the Government could survive only for two and a half years and the Socialist Party faced a big shock.

Janta Dal came into being in 1989. The defunct factions of Janta Party and the defunct groups of Congress joined it. They compromised over the distribution of seats with Bhartiya Janta Party and they took the cooperation of the Communist Parties and other opposition parties. Janta Dal formed a coalition government but the government broke down in 1990 and it was a further loss of the socialist party. When some posts in Government were offered to some socialists, they were feeling honoured with it but it affects adversely to the principles of the socialists. Still so many factions of socialists are scattered throughout the country. It is very much required that they might unite at one platform so the dream of Lohia may be realized in reality.

Development of Backward Classes

According to Lohia, "As socialism would usher in social

and economic equality of people, the development of backward sections and religious minorities is urgently required". He was of the view that without provision for special opportunities, these backward sections could not grow. He was in favour of granting them 60 per cent reservation, so that they may be brought at par with upper sections of the society. These backward classes constitute 90 per cent population in India but occupying only 5 to 10 per cent placements on the higher posts. The other means to bring them at par with higher classes is inter-caste marriage and arrangement for the common meals in certain areas, two times in a year. In this way he suggested practical solutions to the problem of inequality.

According to him, "The age-old debts which are transferred from one generation to another is also one of the reasons for the backwardness of the majority of Indians. These people are born in debt, live in debt and die in debt". He suggested that tribesmen, agricultural labourers and the women who were having no other jobs should be set free from their old debts and, if necessary, the government should make the payment of their debts. He was of the opinion that, "Tribesmen and forests have been the old friends for centuries. Hence, the management of forests should be handed over to the tribesmen and benefit of their knowledge should be sought".

Dr. Lohia realized that the illiteracy was also the major reason for their backwardness. Therefore, he suggested that scholarships and the free hostel facilities should be given to the students belonging to the backward classes. He stressed the need of increasing the number of schools and colleges in backward areas. He also suggested that for this purpose the state governments should provide educational facilities. The government should remove the obstacles in providing the education to the youth of the backward classes. According to him, "when 60 per cent of the seats will be reserved for this section of the society, 10 per cent people of the upper classes will also become conscious because now only 40 per cent seats will be available to them. Initially 10 per cent seats were occupied by 1 per cent of the population but in future 40 per cent seats would be available to 10 per cent people. In this way, the competition would be open and whole of the population would be benefited. He hoped that in future, Indian agriculture would prosper, industries would develop, cooperation between man and man would increase and consciousness of the people would awaken. In this way there would be end of the hunger, caste system and inequality".

He was well aware that people of upper classes would not like this type of equality and would create obstacles against this set-up. He was also aware that if one caste was more benefited it would also create the problem of inequality. Some selfish people would use it for their own benefit and they would oppose each other. Nevertheless, this controversy will not be in the interest of the weaker sections. Thus, it would become an obstacle for the better environment in the society. The provision of reservation for the backward classes was the only way to bring them equal with the upper classes.

He was of the opinion that no child should be deprived of education. Everybody should have equal educational opportunities. Karl Marx also tried to finish the class conflict but he was not aware that this class would turn into another class.

Dr. Lohia said nothing about the old structure of the society rather he only explained about the merits and provisions of equal opportunities of the new prosperous society. He advised the youth of the upper classes that they should become conscious about the fact that the new society would not be antagonistic to them. He was in favour of inter-caste marriages. He advised that the upper classes should consider themselves, as the means for the development of lower classes and in this way, they would also flourish at the same time. When the people of the lower classes would become executives, the members of the upper classes could also become the advisors. Though this system would not be possible everywhere, but it would certainly be possible at maximum places. In this way, the people of upper classes would mix up with the people of the lower classes. He said, "It is also the social responsibility of the members of lower classes that they should not oppose the way of living and the traditions of the upper classes. They should not hesitate to do the manual jobs and they should not think about their own development only. All the people should associate themselves with the better leadership because the development of society was dependent on them".

Seven Revolutions: Those are to be Won

Lohia had suggested seven revolutions for the development of the country as well as for establishment of social equality.

According to him, "For eradication of the social evils", there is a need to launch the following seven revolutions:

1. Equality between men and women.
2. To fight against inequality of political, economic and spiritual nature based on skin and colour.
3. To fight against the inequality between backward and upper classes which is based on the old rituals. It would provide opportunities to members of the backward classes.
4. To fight against the slavery of foreign rule and establishment of democratic set-up in the world.
5. To struggle for ushering in economic equality and increasing production with planning. The provision of private property, but against the deep love for it.
6. To remove the unnecessary interference of the government in the personal lives in a democratic set-up.
7. Against armaments and Agitation.

Dr. Lohia prescribed these revolutions as the objectives of Socialist Party. He wanted that revolution should take place not only in India but also throughout the world. Therefore, he made an appeal to all the citizens of the world that everybody should join this struggle to achieve these objectives. In this way, Lohia wanted to bring peace, democracy, independence, and economic development, end of social evils and creation of an atmosphere of mutual love, cooperation and prosperity throughout the world.

Problems of Women

Dr. Lohia thought that women who could play a very constructive role in any society should be given an honourable status. To deprive them from their right of education and to push them backward in a male dominated society was never desired by Dr. Lohia. In his life, he studied about the status and plight of women in India as well as in various countries of the world. He wanted the end of suppression of women; and desired that women and men should have equal status. According to him, "Women should get equal opportunities like men in all the spheres of life". Once Dr. Lohia said, "I am half a man and a half woman. As long as the sleeping soul of backward classes and women do not awake and efforts are not made for their upheaval and development, no "ism" can infuse new life". Lohia was aware of all problems of women and gave practical suggestions to solve those problems. The suggestions presented by him for their upheaval as well as removal of their difficulties held immense importance. Perhaps he was the first political leader and social reformer of India who suggested construction of latrines for the women. According to him, "Construction of latrines for the women is the primary need of the time. This is not only a problem for the women belonging to villages but also for the women living in cities. In the metropolitan cities of modern era, we do not have the facility of separate latrines for women". While explaining this problem he said "The women who constitute 50 per cent of the society are compelled to ease themselves in the fields either before day dawn or after sunset. If a man wants to urinate, he can do so by standing near a wall but the women have to bear this call of nature for hours". Dr. Lohia thought that this provision of latrines was urgently required for the mental and physical development of women. According to him, "The major reason behind the rising rate of rape of women belonging to backward classes throughout the country was the lack of latrines for them in their houses". As per his views, "It is not a small question. To safeguard the interest of women in the male dominated society is our prime duty whereas no attention has been paid in this direction". Dr. Lohia drew the attention of the society towards this very serious problem of women in India and viewed that under these conditions one could not feel secure. He stressed that "women are suffering from this mental and physical trouble for centuries and no attention was paid to such problems of the society. On the other hand, impracticable solutions are being suggested". Dr. Lohia never liked these unhealthy solutions.

Dr. Lohia raised this matter in Parliament and made the members conscious of about this major as well as serious problem. According to him, "The real meaning of veil is that women should be provided proper place for latrine and bathroom where they can bath freely. On the one side, while people do not care for these two major problems, at the same time on the other hand, they stress that the veil is essential for women". He also made the people cautious about this increasing problem. According to him, "With the passage of time this problem has increased. In ancient times this problem had not been so serious, as people in villages used to go to the fields for answering the call of nature. From the historical facts and old testimonies, it is known that at that time there were no latrines in the houses. This tradition developed with the coming of Muslims, because they wanted that women should remain confined in their houses. Hence, their women could not go outside for latrines". At present, this problem has increased manifold, as there are no fields and forests in towns and cities, similarly, there is less open space in the villages or it is continuously declining, because of the cutting of jungles, there are no more open places in the villages. It has become difficult for the women to find open places to ease themselves also. According to a report in more than 3,000 cities and towns, one-third of the population is not having the facility of latrines. The national average of the people not having latrines in cities is 32.82 per cent so these people make use of the side of road, water channels as latrines. Seventy two per cent of the population is living in villages. The disposal of secreta spread the contagious diseases. Dr. Lohia was the first man to attract the attention of the Members of Parliament towards this serious and most important problem.

According to him, the disposal of excreta in the streets and roads in the open is a crime. The police officials can arrest such a person without any warrant and can present them before the Magistrate. But Lohia attracted the attention of the people as well as the Government of independent India that has failed to provide toilets at the public places. The need of public latrines was the fundamental right of the women for their convenience, social respect and health. However, there was a need to understand the meaning of community health. Here it is very important to understand the human as well as social living.

Dr. Lohia said, "Generally, we compare the women of the ruling class with the common women while, there is great difference in the way of living. It is possible for the women of upper classes to achieve the high positions but a woman of common family cannot even think of it". He suggested that this difference can be understood by other examples. "When we see a woman of upper class in jeans demonstrating her body, she do so for the demonstration of her beauty and pride while the women of poor families are naked for want of sufficient clothes". "On one side, the rich women wear clothes to be naked and on the other side, the women of poor families wear clothes to cover their nakedness." Therefore, he explained the problems of the women in details. While explaining the backwardness of women he said that, "Either a women born in an upper family or in lower family, at both the circumstances their birth is considered a bad omen. In a society where the birth of son is celebrated and the the birth of a girl is considered as a liability it is but natural that the degradation of women starts from the time of their birth."

While deeply going through these psychological problems, Dr. Lohia expressed his views that since ages there had been a tradition that they were dependent and they should be given shelter. He said that drama was still going on and every movement of theirs had been carefully watched. As per Dr. Lohia's views, "Crores of women have to do the manual jobs but still that job is not permanent and the women have to depend on those people who employ them". Here the concept to provide them equal rights seemed to be a joke. Inspite of the legal changes and with the provision of many rights, practically there had been no difference in their position. They are still having the same status, and unemployment is one of the major reasons for them.

After a thorough study on the problems of women, Lohia, found out that inequality of women was also linked with the caste system. He concluded that "In the caste system, the women are given the status of *shudras* (lower classes) while with the spread of the western education it was felt that the discrimination of caste system would finish but it did not happen so as yet. It was on account of the reason that the education had not spread, particularly the girl education remained confined to the girls of upper classes. As the caste system could not be thrown out of the society the problems of the Indian women could not be understood and solved".

In case of late marriage of a girl, instead the girl is criticized. In the same way, if a girl goes out of house after sunset it becomes a problem for that girl. There is a need to awaken the Indian culture where there is no place of such discussion, doubt and the limitations.

Regarding problem of dowry he suggested, "The persons involved in giving as well as taking the dowry should be equally punished. People should change their mindset with regard to the way of life". He was overwhelmed to explain that parents with tears in their eyes had told him that what type of torture was meted to their daughters.

They were beaten up because of fetching less dowry. Literate as well as illiterate both indulged in the dowry. Dr. Lohia suggested that all the political parties of the country, viz., Congress, Communists and Socialists all should chalk out a joint programme for the upliftment of the women. He was also aware of the problems being faced by women in the kitchen. There is a need to install the chimney for the disposal of that dangerous smoke. The women take less food in comparison to the men. The problem of unemployment and less provision of food for women are interlinked and required to be solved. Dr. Lohia realised that the problems of women are multiplied after their marriages.

There are no water taps in the houses so they are destined to fetch dirty and polluted water from the far away wells and ponds. He was of the view that women should launch agitation against this problem. Without large scale movement their problems could not be solved. He also viewed that women should participate in all the struggles.

In his view, "A struggle without the participation of the people of lower classes and the women is incomplete". That is why he was in favour of providing of 60 per cent of reservation to the women and the people belonging to lower castes, harijans, tribesmen, religious minorities and backward classes.

According to Lohia, another reason for the backwardness of women is their tender body on account of that they are beaten and abused. All the abuses are related with women that shows the psychological thinking of male about women and how far backward they are considered.

Dr. Lohia quoted another example of the backwardness of women in India. He said, while looking on the statues of Rani of Jhansi, "We would have to learn something from that". Though big statues of Rani of Jhansi and Panna have been built but both of these have same defects. Rani is positioned on the horseback with a small child on her back. He pointed out that, "I have tried to see that child from all angles with great sympathy. The artist should admit that the statue of Rani could look more beautiful and impressive without the child. What was the need of that child. If it is admitted that while fleeing from the fort the child was tied on the back of Rani but what was the necessity to portray this in stone or some other metal". The Rani would have also rided the horse on other so many occasions. The words written on the statue of Rani are also uncultured. It is written that Laxmi Bai had enhanced the status of Indian women. She had enhanced the status of India. It should also have been written on the statues of Shivaji and Subhash Chander Bose that they had enhanced the status of Indian Men. "Well fought as a male, she was Rani of Jhansi" (*Khoob Lari Mardani woh to Jhansi Wali Rani thi*). From this famous poem, it seems that how art and opinion are interlinked as they are constructed on the basis of male domination. The male mind wants to see Rani with the child.

Another example as quoted by Lohia is that "In Indian houses women take their meals after the males have taken. Therefore, in half fed families, women are to suffer most of the hunger. The crores of women are spoiling their health, while sitting near the hearth with its smoke for hours. At other places the women are to bring water from miles so they are facing social injustice and get the feelings of backwardness and they are psychologically suppressed and this injustice against them is going on throughout the Country".

Therefore, Lohia invites the attention of the people and Members of Parliament towards all the problems of the women and suggested their practical solutions. Although the women were religious, well-wishers and having welfare thinking, but because of the conditions of the society they have been under the will of men folk and in most of the cases, they could not get natural and social justice. The socialists should have the responsibility to organize them as a force for revolution and bring about equality between men and women. With this, there would be a change in society and on the other side, everybody would participate in the development of the society and there would be constructive atmosphere. This is a big task. Dr. Lohia had not only given the practical suggestion, for the change of society but also struggled for that.

Fanaticism

Lohia had equal respect for every religion. He was against fanaticism of every religion. Particularly he did not like such religious feelings where there was hatred for other religions, and propaganda for hatred was being made. He felt that everybody could have his own religious faith. According to him, there is a significant role of religion in everybody's life. People of different religious faiths are living in India as Hindu, Bodhi, Muslim, Sikh, Christians, Jaini, Parsi, etc. The highest number is that of the Hindus that is about 82 per cent of the total population. There had been much scuffles, conflicts and wars because of religions to the extent that religion was the basis of the division of the country. On one side of the line, there are people of one religion and on the other side people of the other religion are there.

In the history of the world, the biggest division of population was made on the basis of religion, Muslims, remained in Pakistan. But it is interesting that even after this division, the largest number of Muslims is still living in India though its division was made on this basis.

Dr. Lohia was not in favour of this division. In his programme, he preached to acquire religious tolerance, respect, love, regard for the feelings of every religion and called to make struggle against fanaticism of any religion. He was saying that I had not seen God but when the need would have, I would feel him without seeing him. Here one point is very interesting and strange also that Lohia had not accepted the concept of God in his life, however, in spite of that he was a true religious and spiritual person. He preached only that what should be the dealing of a person of any religion. He said, "Religion is long time politics and politics is a short time religion". He was feeling that there is such selfishness, greed and race to get the petty gains that neither the religion is being understood nor the politics. According to Lohia if politics is short term religion, so it means that society may be changed with it and it may be a method to change the society and there should not be selfishness, dishonesty, untruthfulness and greed. There may be political, economic and social equality. He was realizing that there is a large number of people in the ruling class those are having the objective to fulfil their own interests. That is why he could permit 49 per cent of self-interest but 51 per cent should be the service of the society.

Dr. Lohia was of the view that liberalism in religion is very essential for development. He was for the Hindu-Muslim Unity. He was saying that Hindu should be half Hindu and Muslim should be a half Muslim. According to him, "Only liberalism can bring unity in the country, India is an ancient and very large country without the human will no other power can bring unity in it. The fanatic Hindu cannot create such will. A liberal Hindu can do it, as he had done earlier". So Dr. Lohia advised Hindus those were in majority that they should show the behaviour of liberalism. The fight of the last 5,000 years has reached to the stage that in political life and as a form of rule, the liberalism in Hindu religion should have victory over fanaticism. He gave so many examples about liberalism from the history of the country and from international history and proved that the religious liberalism is an essential condition for peace, development and solidarity. According to him, I would like to remind the American civil war, where 4 lakh of brothers killed the brothers. At the time of victory, Abrahim Lincoln and Americans showed the same emotional unity between northern and southern brothers. What may be the future of India? The

Hindu religion must change themselves in full and must have to achieve the same emotional unity with Muslims. So, Dr. Lohia was a far-sighted statesman he was having deep understanding about history and human psychology. Therefore, he laid more stress to make the Hindus to understand their responsibility that they may adopt liberalism in their practical life.

According to Lohia, to fight against fanaticism, there is a need to fight at three fronts that is fanaticism front, to believe in caste system front and self-egoism front. He was of the opinion that the problem of fanaticism is growing in India from the last 5,000 years and it is a historical truth that India could not achieve prosperity and peace with fanaticism. Whenever the liberalism took power, the prosperity and unity had been achieved. The tolerance also born with liberalism. As there are different religions in India and the people of different religions should live together with love and cooperation. According to Lohia, fanaticism disappears and it came to its climax only when there is deterioration in the society. There should be no compromise with fanaticism because with this the old blunders would be repeated.

Dr. Lohia respects the people of all the religions but he was against the fanaticism of any religion. As he wished the international peace and the development of democracy at all levels so he was against fanaticism of any religion. According to him, in search to attain power from the principles of anti-democratic principles that is based on the views of caste system and leadership, the fanatic aspect of Hindu religion can wear the clothes of anti-religion.

India is a country of many religious faiths. All communities had been living cordially with good relations with each other. It was based on tolerance. However, the Britishers had encouraged the fanaticism. Their objective behind was the need to rule over India for a very long time. The division of the country based on religion is a clear proof that fanaticism in India was because of colonialism. After independence, according to the Constitution of India, India will be a secular country. There will be no interference in any religion and every religion will be equally respected. On secularism, the views of Lohia were very important and those were based on reality. According to him secularism does not mean to be secular and rather it should mean "Public secularism". Secular means that there is no religion of the state, the state is neither in favour of one religion nor against the other religion. According to him the leaders of the country calls the state as neutral to religion but not to society. However, according to Lohia if the society is not neutral from religion, the state cannot be neutral from religion. To make the society neutral to religion, there should be homogeneous laws in the society. In this pro-public society, social welfare would be promoted for all male and female in the same way.

Lohia faced the opposition from the people holding fanatic religious views. But he has expressed that the leaders have not talked to establish pro-people society. That is why, that though India is a secular country but its form is not as neutral to religions as dreamt by Lohia. Rather some political leaders are using the religious feelings for their petty interests. Dr. Lohia narrated the real situation of the society.

He wrote a book in which he explained about the great Ram, Krishan and Shiv, The great three names. The real explanation is given by him, is rarely available elsewhere. He wrote in it, "What can be the more feelings of truth that from the fifty or one hundred centuries their life is being written in the mind of every dynasty. They are mixed in the sufferings and pleasures of lakhs and crores". Ram, Krishan and Shiva are all over India on the lips of every person and their words, they had spoken at some particular times, every Indian is familiar with them. There is a need for their religious utility in whole of the country because the spiritual path as shown by these people was ideal for everyone. The story of *Ramayana*, *Mahabharta* and life of mother Parvati is the story of the unity of whole of India.

Dr. Lohia explained the fanaticism in his book "Hindi *versus* Hindu." He was of the firm belief that there was no other way for India than to be neutral to religion. According to him, the deterioration is there in all the religions of India at their practical level. According to Dr. Lohia, as 82 per cent are Hindus and if Hindu became fanatic it can spoil whole of the nation because of their being rigid can change the administration of the country. There can be other type of rule than democracy and it can get the minorities away from the national and social life. On the other side, if minorities became fanatic they would separate themselves from the nation and society. So Dr. Lohia preached against fanaticism and in favour of liberalism repeatedly and he explained with farsightedness that it could help the development and unity of the country. It would promote peace and strengthen the country.

To fight against fanaticism, he told about the other struggle that is to fight against the caste system. According to him, till there is caste system in India, there cannot be atmosphere of equality. He expressed his views that fanatic powers are against changes. They hope caste system continues. They consider it a status of Hindus. Whenever there is attack on caste system they succeeded in creating the clashes in Hindu-Muslims, on the pretext to serve religion. He gives different measures to finish caste system. Among them, one is reservation and this is a practical solution. As there are special help plans to develop backward areas, similarly to bring the backward classes in the national stream there should be reservation. He also told about the problems to implement it. According to him if it is implemented strictly it would hurt the special privileges of upper classes. He invites the attention of the people that some of the parties had been in favour for continuing the caste system. There are certain powers against the neutrality of religion on sound basis, therefore, it is essential to identify those powers and such forces may be defeated.

The third front to fight fanaticism is to fight against the individual proprietorship of the wealth. Until there is a control of the capitalists on the sources of the country, the exploitation cannot be finished. The common man is exploited and under this exploitation the capitalist adopts the policy to "create difference" "Divide and Rule". According to him the religious conflicts are excited from upper classes and lower sections of the society considers it proper because of their ignorance. So, if there is equality in the society, this problem can be solved to the large extent. The social equality cannot be established without economic equality.

The political path as explained by Lohia was based purely on truth, justice, and equality. He did not want any demonstration and inequality in the society. Though he was a socialist, but his views were religious. He never wished injustice and inequality that is why his views about religion were very much important. As he said that "Religion is long period politics and politics is short term religion" It carries very deep meaning. He does mean that politics is not a profession, but a means for social welfare where there is no selfish interest. He was worried over the deterioration that has come in the society, where neither the politics is being understood completely nor the religion. Politics is considered as a profession in the modern age. We clearly understand that if self-interest is deleted from the politics, then it becomes a worship and a path for public welfare.

Although India was declared a secular country, yet some parties make the use of religion for their political ends. Some of the parties have brought religious issues in their political programmes. Inequality has increased and equal opportunities for employment could not be available. Corruption has increased. The Socialist Party has cautioned about this inequality repeatedly but it had not achieved much. It does mean that self-interest had remained in politics, that had created many problems and this inequality had encouraged the fanaticism.

It was very interesting that some parties were making

the maximum use of religion for their political ends, but they never admitted that they are using religious sentiments. Every party claims to be the most secular party. Dr. Lohia had made conscious about this. The parties had been using caste system for political ends, Lohia's views had proved much true.

Objectives of Socialist Party

There were so many people in Congress Party, those were having socialist thinking, they desired to establish socialism, where there may be social and economic equality. They desired some fundamental changes in the society, those may be useful for the economic development. There would be prosperity in the society and everybody would get equal opportunities. In the Congress Party, they wished to attain these objectives through Congress Party. The large number among them were the people who had studied in the Indian and foreign universities and they were impressed by socialism. These people organized Congress Socialist section within the Congress in 1934. Later on, some other people joined them but it was very interesting that at the time of their test and struggle, they left socialism. Dr. Ram Manohar Lohia had studied at Calcutta, Bombay, Benaras and Berlin. When he was a student at Berlin, the fascism of Hitler on the one side and communism of Stalin on the other side were at their climax. Lohia was preparing for his doctorate under the guidance of a famous economist of that time Dr. Jambast. During his stay in Germany, he tried to learn very deeply about socialism and imperialism. After returning to India, he had been editing a journal of

Congress Socialist Party that was preaching and advocating the principles of socialism.

It has been a weakness of the party that since the beginning it had been facing the crisis of leadership up to 1949. Mr. Jaya Prakash Narayan was the leader of this group. In those days, Soviet Union was progressing well in their economy under the leadership of Communist Party, it was a matter of discussion and attraction throughout the world. Pt. Jawahar Lal Nehru was a leader of progressive thinking. Since 1936, he was having very good relations with communists, but at that time the Assemblies of Kerala, Tamil Nadu and Andhra Pradesh went out of the socialists and they were occupied by communists. Communists were progressing well with lot of propaganda. Mr. Shankria and Namboodripad, who were the prominent office bearers of Congress Socialist Group went with communists and in this way the tradition to get away from the socialists continued. The socialists had played a big role in winning the independence in India. In 1942, they played a big role to prepare Gandhiji for the struggle.

In 1947, India became independent. The people of socialist group thought that now their path is quite clear and they would establish the socialist society very easily. But within the short time, it became clear that to achieve their objectives is not only far away for them but even the ruling party of that time, Congress is not willing to adopt their issues, so the people belonging to socialist group desired to float a new party as Socialist Party. In 1948, when Socialist Party was organized, Dr. Ram Manohar Lohia was against it because he was of the view that India has become independent after centuries and they should strengthen it in united way. But when his views were not listened in Congress he also got separation from Congress and joined Socialist Party. In 1957-58, Dr. Lohia repeatedly explained the principles of equality of the party. According to him the main objectives of Socialist Party should be to establish a society without discrimination of group and caste and having equality. The other objectives of the party were to remove English, fix wages, break caste system, decrease the limit of expenditure, save Himalayas, the special privileges for Harijans, backward classes and minorities and special opportunities for the poor of the upper classes, etc. The principle of special opportunities is separate from reservation. Reservation strengthens caste system. Socialist Party was having its separate position. They suggested very constructive and practical solutions.

The objectives of socialism were according to the views of Dr. Ram Manohar Lohia and these were very essential for prosperity of the Indian society. These objectives are Nationalism, Democracy, Socialism, Casteless and Sectionless society and these objectives were to be achieved by peaceful means. According to Lohia there is a need to separate the objective of attaining power only by the politicians but the party should continue with the struggles and constructive work till the objectives are achieved. Vote, jail and constructive work are the three means to achieve the objectives of socialism.

In 1967, Congress lost elections in many states because of the criticism of the Congress as a ruling party. However, Lohia considered it a very small achievement in view of his big goals. For his views on complete revolution and to establish complete economic equality he suggested some goals as the minimum and maximum wages and expenditure and this difference should not be more than 10 times. According to the basis of prices at that time, it should not be less than Rs. 100 and not more than Rs. 1,000 and his slogan became popular throughout the country. He talked about special privileges for equality on the social front. He talked about reservation for Harijans, tribals, women, backward classes, without any religious differences in administration, education, services, trade and even 60 per cent reservation in political offices. He was in favour of the policy of decentralization in which he advocated the four pillar administrations. He was to take strict steps to finish corruption. According to him education is essential for the success of democracy. He advocated the non-alignment and not to join the American or Soviet Union group. To establish peace in Indian sub-continent, he recommended to establish Indo-Pak Confederation. With the elections, the Government changes from one party to another but it does not change the society. It is required to change the thinking and trend of the people for the change of social structure. He launched so many movements and demonstrations under the Socialist Party for the change in the social structure. Though thousands of people went to jail but it changed the thinking of the people and people realized the basis of socialism.

The socialists made use of their power to the maximum between 1946 and 1952. The socialists were having good image in the labourers of Bombay. The labourers launched an agitation and this agitation continued for two months. In the municipal elections of 1947, socialists occupied all the seats but in 1952 they lost all the seats very badly and the same happened after the strike of 1974 at the national level. In the strike of 1974, this party was dependent on other parties. whenever the socialist joined any group of parties they lost later on. They made a joint front with communists in 1936 and an agreement with Dr. Ambedkar regarding seats. After losing the elections of 1952, they made an agreement with Kissan Mazdoor Party but that could not continue for 5 years. In 1953, some victories could be achieved but after that the efforts were made for an compromise with Nehruji but success could not be achieved. As a result, the Socialist Party got sick with those compromises and pessimism prevailed among the workers and leaders of the party.

Dr. Lohia was not in favour of such compromises and agreements and he could not make any agreement just to attain power. What he was saying he was doing it and he was preaching only that, that he was doing and he was never in favour to achieve the selfish ends with the politics that may be of any type. He did not want to arrive at any such compromise that may harm his principles and the growth of the thought may be obstructed. So often he talked to walk alone and after such failures, he decided to walk alone and he advocated his principles as vote, jail and constructive work for his success.

Dr. Lohia's main objective was to achieve seven revolutions and there was a need of struggle to achieve these objectives. He wished to see socialism throughout the world and democracy at all the levels. In the Quit India Movement, Ram Manohar was the main hero. He was a close associate of Gandhiji and Nehruji in the struggle of freedom. When he tried to organize a socialist group in the Congress with his associates Jaya Prakash Narayan and Narender Dev, he had to face opposition within the Congress Party. When Dr. Lohia left the party and form Socialist Party but still he found that his friends Ashok Mehta and Jaya Prakash Narayan had the policy of coordination with Congress. So he decided to go alone and he named his party as "Praja Socialist Party and expressed the hope that they would attain power in seven years and would continue their struggle for 100 years. He wished that the money spent on wars in this world should be spent on the development of backward countries and for the human welfare. He opined that world parliament and world government should be elected by adult franchise. He was of the opinion that the promise of Pt. Jawahar Lal Nehru to establish socialistic pattern of society is just a delusion. He was in favour to take solid steps to establish socialism.

Removal of English

Dr. Lohia was not in favour of the continuous use of English. He was advocating the use of local languages. According to him the Central Government was guilty of making the use of English continuously. He gives his view that democracy should be real and the language of the people is its second name. The talking in English should be finished and children should be imparted education in their mother tongue. Here again he was against the people who supported continuation of English and those had controlled the jobs. According to him to ignore the language of the people is to finish the soul of India. He was of the opinion that the people of upper classes and rich people are making the use of English, the people of upper classes cannot give its solution, and when somebody else gives its solution, they becomes against it. According to him, mother tongue should be used at the provincial level and Hindi and other languages should be used at the centre. The continuous use of the language that is not understood, the people grows weak. He quoted the examples of China and Japan, where their technical knowledge is imparted in their own languages. They had developed their technical ability to the higher level. According to him in India there is an influence of three elements, these are money, English language and upper classes and these had created the obstacles in the development of the country. He believed that the medium of education should be their mother tongue. Democracy can develop if their education is in their mother tongue.

India-Pakistan Confederation

Dr. Lohia and his party were not in favour of the division of the country. They were always interested for Hindu-Muslim unity and unity among the people of all the religions. They never wanted that country might be divided on the basis of religion. However, once they could not check it, India became independent but it was divided as two countries—India and Pakistan. Once the country was divided, Dr. Lohia suggested the confederation of India and Pakistan for the peace, and economic development of both the countries. According to him, there is a situation of everything and nothing in the relations of India and Pakistan. Kashmir or any other problem cannot be solved at its own. We should have the courage to see that division has not solved the problem for which it was divided. So unity between India and Pakistan has again become essential, it might be in any form. There is a little importance that this unity may be called federation or confederation. Let us in the beginning it may be called confederation. Everybody knows that confederation is just a traditional administration and it will be turned into federation and it will dissolve after some time.

Lohia said, he knows that his idea would not be liked by so many people though some of the people liked confederation, I may request them that they may think their alternatives. It is essential that there may be unity in India and Pakistan that may be related with these departments as foreign policy, security, communication and currency and similarly on the question of citizenship. Every Muslim and Hindu may feel himself secure. According to him long time would be taken to think on his suggestions and he said that I pray that people and associations may think deeply over these views.

Political Party

Lohia was of the view that the membership should continue throughout the year. Every active member should enroll 20 ordinary members. These 20 members should be intimated about the policies of the party. Every political matter should be discussed with them. Their suggestions should be listened, and these should be discussed. These suggestions should be sent to the National Executive of the party. It is quite possible that these suggestions may be appreciated by the national executive and may be useful for the society. He criticized the procedure of membership as adopted in these days. The ordinary members are not even informed that they are being enrolled as members, what they can contribute in the social and political life and how the targets can be achieved. According to Dr. Lohia, Now our ordinary member is having no job just after signing, something else is not expected from him. These members should use their rights. In these days these members are not informed about anything to the extent that no need of these members arises in the elections of the representatives, some of the members just sit in a room and completes the process of elections, in the bars of falsehood and self-hypocrisy.

Here one thing is essential to state that the people of the other parties know this truth and they are doing this. Even the signatures of the ordinary members are not taken and further to the extent that the ordinary charges are not being taken and the active members themselves pay the charges and in this way, the membership is completed. Dr. Lohia was much against this type of membership and what is the meaning of such a membership, where the members are not joining the party with heart and brain, how they can accept the view-point of the party and it is all the foundation of falsehood. Dr. Lohia understood this problem from its depth and he was to remove such a practice. He was never dependent on such a bogus membership and it can cause a big loss in future instead of gaining. He was of the opinion that the elections should start from the ordinary members. In this way, the ordinary member would suppose that he is also involved in the party/programme and policies and his interest in party would increase. The meetings of ordinary members should be held at proper intervals. Though it is not possible at the central level, but these can be arranged at the local level in every area. Discussions should be held in such meetings, suggestions should be taken and resolutions should be passed. Only then the socialistic pattern can be established and everyone would feel that he is a partner in it when they would pass some resolution or they would reject it, the party leadership would get guidance. Lohia felt that from the ordinary member to the President of the party, the party belongs to everyone, and everyone has the right to participate and he could give suggestions. In other words there would be a feeling of equality for everyone. According to Lohia there should be meetings of the ordinary members, twice in the area. All the questions should be discussed in this meeting. The ordinary members should pass resolutions. There should be no check on these resolutions, because according to Constitution their importance can be in the advisory form only while discussing and passing of resolutions the members would realize widening of their vision and freedom, and they would feel that they are the partners in the policy making of the party. According to Dr. Lohia when any party comes in power it also use the same methods as the previous parties were using. But he was of the view that the base of the party should be from the lower level.

People would listen my views but ....?

Dr. Lohia said it correctly, that "People would pay attention to my views but after my death. Dr. Lohia said it in 1962 in the session at Nagarjun Sagar in a public rally. At that time, Lohia had become much popular in India and at the international level. Some of his issues like man-woman equality, social and economic equality, sectionless and casteless society, and democracy throughout the world and at all levels, social equality throughout the world were much appreciated. He suggested the continuous struggle to achieve these objectives. He advised his followers to be away from the politics of self-interest that is why still his followers, though they took part in freedom struggle, they did not avail pensions or other benefits because they believed in politics that is away from the personal interest. His struggle was not for a particular area or for particular people but it was for the humanity. His views were very correct that any ism if it is not for humanism cannot prolong. He never compromises at the cost of principles. He did not make any demonstration, nor created any artificial drama, though he had to suffer a lot or he had to face insult. As Gandhiji dreamt for "Ram Raj" Dr. Lohia dreamt for "Sita Ram Raj" that means that women should be given equal status and respect in the society.

As it happens that every thinker has to pay the price for his views similarly he had to go to jail for his views. He had gone to the jail in the British rule as well as in the independent India, jail under Portugal Rule and jail in Nepal rule and jail in America. But he was prepared to pay any price for his ideals. He said, once someone asks Mr. Lenin that why you spoke so sour and Lenin replied that where the fire of sufferings of the exploited people is burning all the time, how he can speak sweet. Similarly, Lohia said, "Till the socialists have not decided with heavy heart that we are to advocate the politics of lower classes of the society, farmers, labourers, students and to run the movements of labourers, agricultural labourers, farmers, women, break down of caste, nothing, can be achieved. We may achieve success or failure. This is the politics that we are to practise. Until you had not decided solidly, your mind will be attracted towards this mean politics".

Actually, the seven movements as suggested by Dr. Lohia are the solution of the problems of all the countries of the world. In a country, where there is need of economic and social equality and where the society is having no caste and creed system, democracy can be a big success. The fixation of limit of income and expenditure is required. The light of education should spread and there should be unity among the whole society of the world. where there is no complication and no war, no controversy there should be spirit of cooperation and brotherhood, there should be equal and similar privileges and laws for everyone and there should be good moral values. These were the principles around which the views of Dr. Lohia had been surrounded and he had been struggling to achieve his objectives. That is why he said, people would listen him but after his death and it is correct also that now the people are not only listening his views but even applying them in their programmes. These are not only members of the socialist parties but non-socialist parties also who are considering themselves as the real followers of Dr. Lohia.

He was well-understanding the psychology of the Indian mind. He was realizing that the people desired to get the results at the earliest. They cannot prolong their struggle for long time. He said, There is anxiousness, hurry and self-interest in the suppressed and lower classes. They wish to achieve everything at the earliest. They wish to get ahead immediately. If you get us advanced, then it is all right, otherwise we are leaving you and they leave also. But as Lohia was aware about this psychology and he was not pessimist about that and nor he felt it a weakness of the people. He was having his sympathy for their helplessness.

According to Dr. Lohia, party workers should accept the principles from heart and they should continue their efforts to achieve these goals continuously. To establish the socialist structure its benefits should be explained everyday. The foundation of the party is its members. Every year the membership is filled before the annual session and it is completed before the session for a year. There is a tradition to fill the members as sheep and goats. There is a fear to fill the fake members and the members whose names are filled in this way cannot form an organization for revolutionary struggles.

He has studied the functioning of the political parties of India, and he was against the fake membership. His politics was based on sound views. There should be cooperation with heart and brain in political struggles, only then the society can be changed and a socialistic pattern can be established. According to Dr. Lohia, only to gather the crowd at particular time and to get the cooperation of 20-25 thousands of persons at the time of agitation cannot serve the purpose. The party does not become familiar with public. The real power in party can be only if the membership continues throughout the year and people may become the member being familiar to the programme and policy of the party.

He was feeling that maximum people may know the party programme and about the objectives to establish the socialistic pattern of society. The ordinary members should also be aware and active members of the party should have knowledge not only about their country but with the situation of whole of the world. They should talk with other parties and while discussing with other parties, they should have wide knowledge, so they may not feel any weakness at any time. All that shows that he did not believe in vain arguments and fake promises, what he was propagating, he was doing that.

He was a man of determination and strong views. He never fear for his criticism and nor backtracked in the struggle to achieve his objectives. He expressed that now as independence is achieved, a new society would be organized. However, when he saw that it is not being achieved, what he thought before independence, he took his own path. He could get any political office, but he was determined that there should not be any self-interest in politics and he proved it that he was a far-sighted statesman who was much above from the personal interest.

Index